THE ORIGIN & NATURE OF THE

TROPICAL ZODIAC

The zodiac signs: what they are and who created them. Ptolemy and the Inherent Zodiac

Written in simple, non-technical language with clear graphics, this book provides an authoritative explanation of the origin and validity of the zodiac signs. With extracts from key ancient Greek texts, translated by the author.

DAMIEN PRYOR

Threshold Publishing
sales@insearchofknowing.com

ISBN 978-0-9581341-3-2

CONTENTS

Chapter One

Introduction: the big questions

Almost nothing can be found in any book that explains what the zodiac signs actually are. Are the zodiac signs that are used in a horoscope valid? Since they are not the constellations of the zodiac, but form some kind of invisible zodiac, what are they? If they exist, where are they? Is astrology based on a nonsensical, indeed non-existent ghost zodiac so to speak? Are the astronomers right, that there should be 13 zodiac signs, because there are 13 constellations in the zodiac? Are those astrologers correct, who draw up a horoscope based on where the sun and the planets are situated amongst the visible stars (sidereal zodiac)?

Have the zodiac signs been drifting apart from the constellations, or do they not even exist out there in space at all? And how important are the ancient Babylonian zodiac signs? Did the ancient authority, Claudius Ptolemy, (ca. 130-140 AD) ever really state that the zodiac should be moved, or be kept fixed? What did the ancient astrologer sages, informed by the Mysteries, say about the zodiac signs?

These are questions which up to now have not been clearly answered. This booklet will endeavor to answer these questions, and it will be a really easy booklet to read! I shall not be using any technical, confusing specialist terms! (Any such terms that have to be mentioned, will be clearly explained or put into end-notes.)

The reader may already know that when you have a horoscope drawn up, and you see the planets located in various **Signs** which are named after the constellations, such as Gemini or Taurus, these signs belong to a zodiac which is not the same as the zodiac made up of the **Constellations** of stars. And this implies that there are two zodiacs; one made up of signs, the other made up of constellations. The Horoscope Signs zodiac is a 12-fold circle in which each division is of the same size, but these divisions or signs are not in the same place as the unequal-sized star constellations, after which each is named, see illustration 1.

This shows very clearly just how different is the personality, if you assess the client using the constellations zodiac or the tropical zodiac.

For example, if the sun is in the Sign of Taurus, then that person (bearing in mind that there are about 20 elements to interpreting a chart) will be a more earth-related type, fond of gardening and the land, and slow to excitement or anger or rapid activity.

However, if you look where the sign of Taurus is located, then beyond it, you will see the stars of the constellation of the Ram, called Aries. The illustration will show that each of the zodiac signs are in a different place in the heavens to the zodiac constellation of the same name.

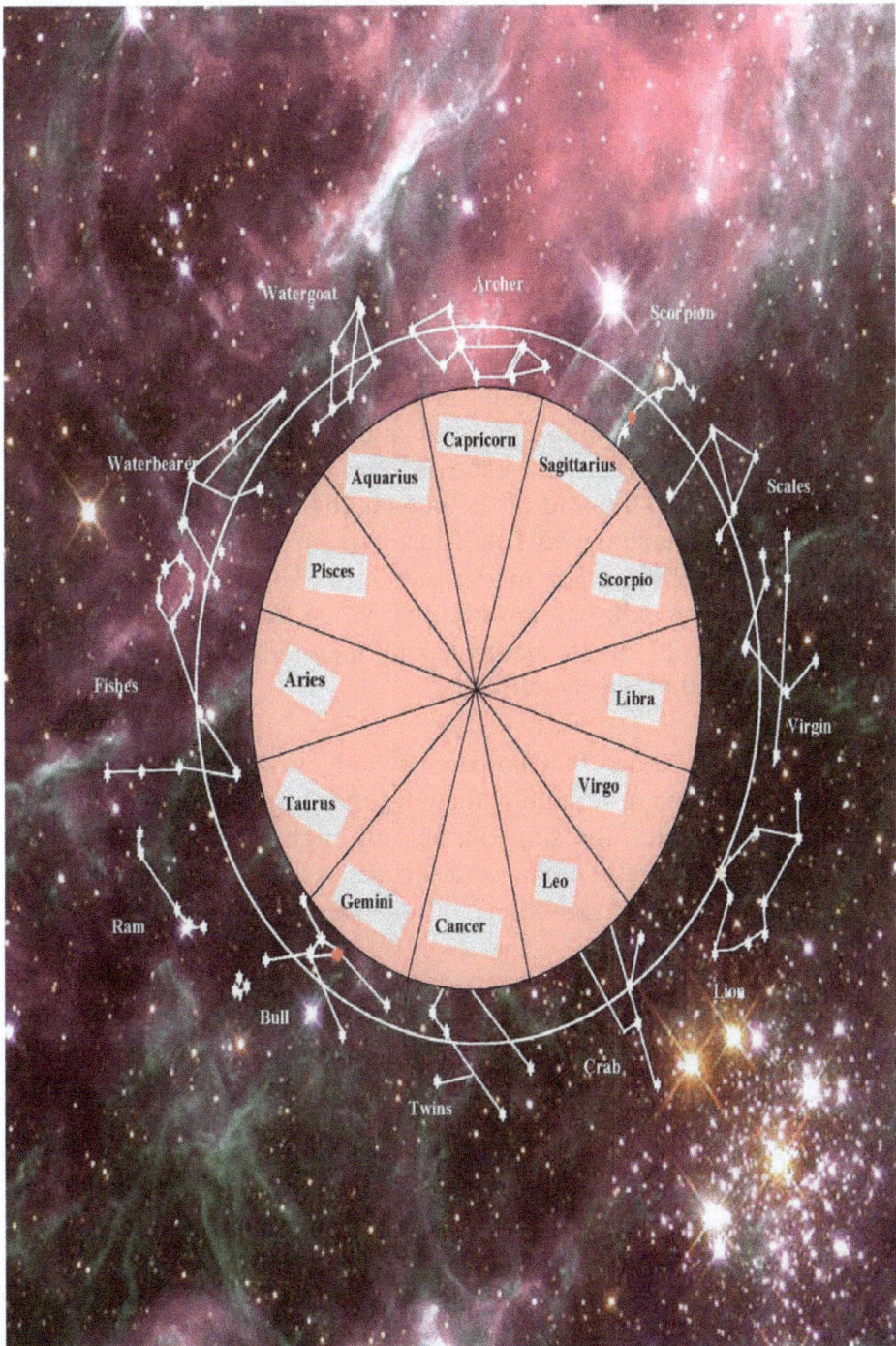

1 The zodiac Signs and the zodiac constellations. The Signs (in pink) are not aligned with the constellations. Thus a 'Taurean' person was born when the sun was actually amidst the stars of Aries the Ram, and so on.

So, if one uses the star-based zodiac (known as the *sidereal* zodiac), then the same person will be defined as an Aries personality. And then the person should have totally different qualities, such as a fiery dynamism, a competitiveness, and so on. However, and this is the key point, they won't be an Aries type at all! They will be a Taurean type.

But remember, when assessing a personality, there is also what we call the Rising Sign. This is the sign (or sector) that is on the eastern horizon when the babe is born. This sign is of equal influence in the structure of the personality to the sun-sign, so if you know a person who has Taurus or an Aries as their sun-sign, but who does not match either of these brief simplistic outlines very much, rest assured that when the Rising Sign and all the other 20 or so elements are factored in, they will be accurately and precisely defined.

This diagram shows the horoscope with its zodiac signs (the inner circle) and around this, the circle of the star formations or constellations that the sun journeys through. We can call this the Constellational Zodiac; and we can see that its star-groups are not aligned to the Signs of the same name.

But if this diagram were made 2,000 years ago, the inner circle (the horoscope zodiac) would be moved backwards about a small amount, and if it were made for 3,000AD the inner circle would have to be moved forwards a small amount. Because the zodiac constellations and this 'invisible' zodiac are constantly moving apart.

We shall find out why this happens, and that it is not due simply to "the precession of the equinoxes". The sun does slip backwards (or precess) through the different sectors of the heavens over many centuries. That is an astronomical fact, which will be explained clearly, later. But how can some kind of invisible zodiac, made up of zodiac signs, be moving? We need to know more about the origin of the zodiac before we can answer these questions.

More than one Zodiac?

As we explore the nature of the zodiac used in a horoscope, a new realization will emerge:

there is no such thing as "the zodiac". There are <u>several</u> zodiacs involved. This is not always clear to astronomers and astrologers.

These zodiacs will be clearly explained in the accompanying graphics. So, what are the so-called zodiac signs as used in the horoscope?

Why twelve months and twelve constellations?

Let's leave behind the confusing ideas about the zodiac signs, and see what leading spiritual thinkers of the ancient cultures tell us about them. These are the people who gave us the zodiac constellations and the zodiac signs. Once we know what these people say, we shall be in a position to better understand what these zodiac signs really are.

First, let's look at a really simple question, with an open mind; how many months in the year are there? Well, as we know, there are twelve. But, <u>why</u> are there twelve? Where does that number come from? Experts in the history of astronomy can tell us that historically this comes from ancient cultures, from ancient Babylonia in particular. But these historians cannot actually tell us why these ancient star-gazers established <u>twelve</u> months to each year.

Academic experts in the history of astronomy such as Van der Waerden, Francesca Rochberg, David Pingree and Otto Neugebauer are unable to make a firm conclusion about why this was done. But it is known that before 1000 BC, and possibly back as far as 3000 BC already, in Mesopotamia, the year was divided into twelve months, each of 30 days.[i] And likewise the ancient Egyptians in this same epoch, divided the year into twelve months of 30 days. (They also subdivided these into three equal parts, called decans.)

Let's be clear that a year is the time it takes for the sun to journey around the sphere of stars that encircle the Earth. In other words, if the ancients noted the position of the sun amongst some stars on a certain day, they would see that it takes 365 days for it to appear amongst the same stars. When the ancient peoples established their system of twelve months, each month was given 30 days. This is of course just five days short of the actual 365 days involved.

Some scholars believe that this choice of the number twelve derives from the fact that ancient people often had a strong lunar focus, as they were aware that there are 12.4 lunar months in a solar year. That is, the moon goes through a bit more than 12 of its twenty eight day cycle during one year. But other scholars have concluded that the twelve months of the year are not derived from this lunar cycle, because of the difficulty involved in harmonizing the lunar months with the actual length of the year. Although it is true that some cultures did have a lunar based calendar, others opted for a simpler solar-based calendar, because it only needed minor adjustments.

A lunar calendar eventually leads to major problems with sacred festivals that are based on the sun's yearly cycle. The early Babylonian and Egyptian cultures had festivals linked to the cycle of the year that is, the sun's journey around the Earth. But if they used a lunar calendar, a festival for the spring equinox or the winter solstice could be easily celebrated at the wrong time, unless a complex adjustment system was used to add in the missing days. As the website *Calendars through the Ages* tells us, this system required the addition of an extra month three times every eight years, and as a further adjustment, the king would periodically order the insertion of an additional extra month into the calendar. (1)

We can conclude that therefore the sun's movement throughout the year was a primary focus of these ancient civilizations, and from this they created a twelve-month year. Scholars are not sure what kind of markers were decided upon throughout the sun's journey by the ancient star-gazers, to get to the number twelve. However, the ancient star-gazers did decide to divide the year into twelve months of 30 days each.

And this collection of months produces in total 360 days, and so it nearly equals the length of the year (they knew to add five extra days). But the situation is that the reason for twelve months remains a mystery. The question arises now; can the reason be connected to the zodiac, since it has twelve constellations? The answer is: perhaps, and perhaps not. Because around 3,000 BC these civilizations already had the year divided up into these twelve months, but it was not until 500 BC that the Babylonians records show a twelve-fold zodiac. So most authorities conclude that there is no connection between the zodiac and the 12 month year, since 2,500 years elapse before the twelve-fold zodiac appears. But, the possibility remains that there may be a connection, we shall explore this later on.

Are there 13 zodiac constellations ?
Now let's look again at that other really intriguing question, and see if it can be answered. Why did the ancients decide that there are twelve constellations of stars encompassing the path of the sun around the Earth? Why in the circuit of the sun around the Earth in one year does it go through twelve constellations? Here, of course we are talking about the ancient model of the cosmos, where the Earth is in the centre of the cosmos.

Why didn't they decide on 5 constellations or 8, or perhaps 16 or 27 constellations? Recently various astronomers have again been pointing out that in the classical twelve constellations of the zodiac, which lie on the path of the sun (called the ecliptic) there is actually a small portion of a thirteenth constellation, called the Serpent-Bearer, or Ophiuchus. So these astronomers ask, shouldn't there be thirteen zodiac constellations and therefore, for those who believe in astrology, shouldn't they believe in thirteen zodiac signs? The answer is no, there shouldn't be 13!

We will soon see exactly why. But first let's go back to the far more important question. Why aren't there 7, or 6, or 17 or 51 constellations, or indeed 13 constellations in the classical ancient system? Let's be here clear about this; just take a look at the stars in the night sky. There are hundreds of stars along the path of the sun which are visible in the dark night skies! If someone asked **you** to arrange all of these stars, the ones that lie on the path of the sun, into imaginary images, how many would **you** create? Maybe 19, or maybe 30 or maybe 8? You certainly wouldn't have any reason to create twelve; and certainly not with such figures as a set of weighing scales, or a water-jug bearer, or a lion, or an fantastical water-goat, etc, etc. (Though you might create a scorpion, because the stars of the Scorpion are shaped a bit like one).

In the oldest Babylonian star maps of 4,000 years ago or earlier, there were 18 constellations; and this was a lunar-based system. It showed the star groups through which the moon travels. But as from about 500 BC the later Babylonians decided to create images of twelve constellations, with such images as the Scales, the Water-bearer, etc. So at this time the priests established a sun-based zodiac, not a lunar one. It is an intriguing fact that no ancient documents have been found which prove the existence of the twelve-fold solar zodiac before about 500 BC.

These civilizations from which we get our zodiac system were a type of theocracy, where the head of state was the king or pharaoh who was dependent upon the senior priests and priestesses. The priesthood was a very powerful institution in these ancient cultures that built and maintained massive temples and also vast, majestic tomb complexes. The priesthood celebrated spiritual-religious festivals connected to various seasonal or cosmic influences, etc. In their temples they also carried out complex rituals to do with what is called initiation, that is with experiencing their gods.

It is now academically established that the Egyptians too had their own Mysteries, not only the ancient Babylonians. It is clear that the national focus of the religious life of Babylonia and Egypt was focused on learning about spirit realms, cosmic forces, the significance of the stars, and also of course, about the fate of the soul in the after-life. These ancient institutions, known as *The Mysteries* were like those established in ancient Greece; where the high office bearers were very respected. So, if the priesthood of the Babylonian Mysteries decided upon twelve as the number of solar constellations, and also that these should be imaged as a set of scales, or two fishes, etc, then they must have had substantial reasons to do this. Can we find out what they were?

Summing up so far, we note that we today have twelve months to the year, and we view the starry skies (along the sun's path) as divided up into twelve constellations, because of decisions made by high priests of Babylonia. They concluded that as the sun goes around the Earth every year, so to speak, through vast fields of stars spread out chaotically around us, these star groups should be divided into twelve images.

So what about a possible 13th constellation, called Ophiuchus, the Serpent Bearer? These ancient priests knew about the night sky! If anyone was ever aware of the star groupings around the path of the sun it was these people. And this was millennia before modern astronomers began to map the visible stars. The Serpent Bearer was not included amongst the Babylonian zodiac constellations. It appears about 2,000 years ago in the works of Ptolemy; so it does not belong to the older zodiac constellations. (2)

The reason why twelve not thirteen is correct
The objection that there should be 13 constellations is a totally misleading objection. For as we just noted, there are potentially scores of constellations that anyone could invent; yet the priests had decided upon twelve. Yes, the Serpent Bearer is there, but only as from Ptolemy's time (1st century AD), and yes, a part of the Serpent Bearer does occur amongst the top part of the Scorpion. However, we need to get the true picture here, for that's not all. The sun passes through only a tiny part of the constellation of the Archer (Sagittarius), and likewise a tiny part of the Scorpion (Scorpio).

And, as for the constellation of Aries, the sun passes through almost none of it that we can see! There is one lonely faintly visible star that the sun goes past, for a day or so. Hence about 98% of the visible stars of Aries are away from the sun, quite a distance up above the ecliptic. Aries is hardly amongst these zodiac groups at all. In fact when the sun is said to be going through Aries, the sun is **just as close** to several stars of the non-zodiac constellation of the sea monster called Cetus, as it is to one or two stars of Aries![ii] In old star atlases the artist certainly could draw vivid pictures showing the feet and underbelly of the Ram extending right down to the ecliptic, but actually there are really almost no stars in that area at all, from the Ram.

If you draw a realistic picture, all you could perhaps have is the end of the tail of a lamb down there. **So, it is completely misleading to try to define the number of zodiac constellations by the visible stars**.

So now the first objection is: Why aren't there 14 zodiac signs? How can astrology insist that there are only 12 constellations, when parts of at least two other constellations, Cetus and Ophiuchus, intrude into the zodiac system? And then the second objection has to be: how can astrology insist that there are as many as 12 constellations, when one of the allowed group is

14

almost completely missed out? These are the really crucial questions.

The answer lies in the fact that the actual imagery in the constellations is not the important point at all. They are artistic symbols of an underlying twelve-fold reality. So, the presence of, or the non-presence of, stars in the sun's path is not the important thing.

The reason why Babylonian astrologers defined the zodiac as having twelve constellations is unknown to academic scholars. But we can surely conclude that these ancient star gazers detected (or if you like, believe they detected) **twelve, and only twelve, specific areas out there in space, from which spiritual influences radiated out down onto the Earth. Influences that have a formative impact upon this planet and its inhabitants**.

These were experienced as influences that become activated by the passage of the sun through those areas. The ancient sages clearly detected 12, and not 13 or 30 or 8, or 51 etc, influences. So it is quite irrelevant if a small bit of another constellation intrudes into this area, or if most of a zodiac star group, such as Aries, is almost completely missing in the sun's pathway. But also very importantly, modern psychological astrology also completely confirms that there exist these twelve groups of people, and only these twelve. The twelve zodiac images convey a deep symbolic message about the nature of these twelve influences.

To the ancients, **there are twelve star constellations of relevance to the Earth and humanity**, regardless of how many of their stars are near to, or far from, the ecliptic. And regardless of any intrusion of small parts of other constellations amongst these twelve. And when one works professionally with these twelve, via the horoscope using the zodiac signs, **one finds that the ancients are exactly right**. There are not 13 nor

9 nor 34 influences from the stars, operative in human psychology.

So all the people born whilst the sun goes through the sector (or sign) known as Scorpio, are in fact Scorpios, in their sense-of-self, their personality. There are no snaky Ophichucans amongst them! In fact this truth is the primary proof of the validity of the zodiac signs, as thousands of practitioners working as psychologists or counselors can confirm. It is obvious to the intuitive person, although proof is lacking, that the choice by the ancient Babylonians to have twelve months in a solar year is designed to represent the influence of the twelve zodiac constellations. Now let's see what the problem is regarding the two kinds of astrology.

Chapter Two

Concerning the sidereal and the tropical systems.
For a researcher to work with the night sky, whether a modern astronomer or ancient astrologer, she or he needs to know where a star or planet is, or where it shall be at some time, or where and when the moon or sun rises on a particular day. To achieve this, a system of coordinates is needed of course. That is, a way of locating the planet or star in the sky, to identify the whereabouts of a celestial thing (the sunrise, a planet, the star groups, etc). That really means to identify your location in respect of these things, or their location in respect of your horizon. There are two ways to do this; one is called sidereal, the other is called tropical. These terms are not so difficult, you can easily understand them.

The Sidereal System
The sidereal system takes it name from the Latin word for "of the stars". In the sidereal system (the star-based system) you use the background of the distant fixed stars as a frame of reference. If you do this, you are then using the Celestial Sphere as your frame of reference. The Celestial Sphere is simply the night sky; it appears to be a great upside-down cup of stars, towering above us. It is the sphere of the starry heavens. Ptolemy also used this sidereal system and he specified as primary coordinates, the same two bright stars which the ancient Babylonians used, namely Antares and Aldebaran. They are opposite each other in the heavens, and are found in the constellations of Scorpio and Taurus. So here the moon or sun's movement is plotted against the starry background of the celestial sphere, and not where it is found at an equinox or solstice time.

The Tropical System
The tropical system takes its name from the Greek word for 'turning", meaning the turning point in the sun's journey which will lead to a new season. In the tropical system (the turning-point system) the main coordinate used is the position of the sun

at the Vernal (springtime) Equinox Point, and other key seasonal times. In other words it is a view of which takes the Earth-Sun connection as a basis. So this system is based on the sun's movement as experienced from the Earth during the seasonal cycle.

Thus an important coordinating factor here is the position of the spring equinox; that is where the sunrise occurs on the vernal equinox. This means that the main coordinate is the point of intersection of the sun's pathway (called the ecliptic) with what we call the Celestial Equator. The points where the sun on its apparent path in the sky intersects the Earth's equator, projected out into space, are called nodal points. The Celestial Equator is simply a term for the equator of the Earth, imagined as a huge circle projected outwards from the Equator onto the celestial sphere of stars (like the rings of Saturn).

So, this is not difficult to grasp; these are two ways of identifying the position of something in the heavens. And this simply means that as regards a horoscope, a sidereal chart shows the positions of the planets, etc, with respect to the zodiac constellations. Whereas a tropical chart shows the positions of the planets, etc, with respect to the invisible equal-sized divisions or signs superimposed on the heavens.

And in this system, the beginning of the sign of Aries is placed at a certain set place in the heavens, it does not move. That set place is where the sun rises on the vernal equinox each year. In the time of Claudius Ptolemy this point occurred near the beginning of the stars of Aries. It is this system which has a connection to astrology, since it is this so-called tropical zodiac which is used in our horoscopes. It is a very efficient method, and this general system of coordinates is still used by astronomers today. The letters VP mean Vernal Point, and this phrase itself is an abbreviation for "the point against the starry background where the sun rises on the spring or vernal equinox, being the 21st March in the northern hemisphere". (Vernal is another word for spring.) What is a little more difficult is this.

In the Hellenistic Age, astronomers, especially Hipparchus (ca. 150 BC), discovered that in fact the point where the VP occurs is not actually fixed in terms of the starry background. The background is apparently slowly moving.

Ptolemy and the tropical or sidereal system
And here comes a significant point. The main authority for the zodiac used by astrologers is Claudius Ptolemy, who wrote in the second century AD. He was well aware of Hipparchus, and yet he indicated that a chart's beginning, the sign or sector of Aries (the first sign in the zodiac), is always aligned to where the point where the sun's pathway intersects the Earth's equator (projected out into space). That is, to where the sun is seen to rise on the morning of the spring equinox, see illustration 2.

And he implies that this same point, which is always the beginning of the sign of Aries, should always be used in the future. And so this is the really significant point: the drifting of the star background mentioned by Hipparchus, is actually ignored when a horoscope is drawn up, using the tropical system.

2   The astronomical basis of the tropical zodiac.   The sun on March 21, demarcating the beginning of the sign of Aries.

The tropical zodiac has this name because its first sector (the sign of Aries) starts at the equinox sunrise point, (21st March), at which time the sun turns in its pathway, and moves towards summer. The word for this turning action is "tropical" in Greek. But the tropical zodiac not just a theoretical construct starting at sunrise point on the 21st March; see illustration 5. In green line = the Earth's equator and extended out into space is the celestial equator. The sign of Aries is located where the sun in its pathway (the ecliptic, in yellow) crosses the celestial equator, at March 21st.

Though the stars of Aries or the Ram are no longer in the background when the sun rises on the spring equinox, the sign or sector of Aries is still positioned at the spring equinox point. For Ptolemy indicates that this zodiac should always be positioned with the beginning of the sign of Aries at that same fixed point, even though out in space, the starry background is gradually shifting. That is the initial reason why the tropical chart used by astrologers keeps this same fixed beginning point, and ignores the changing star background.

What this means is in effect that the points where the sun's pathway intersects the Earth's equator at the spring and autumn equinox (projected out into space) take priority, in the tropical zodiac, over the actual moving starry background. When Ptolemy was writing, the spring equinox occurred against the stars of the Ram (Aries in Latin). But not any more, for the stars of the Fishes (Pisces) are to be seen there now. But this tropical zodiac was not unique to Ptolemy, others already had aligned the signs precisely to the solstices and equinoxes, centuries earlier. We shall consider this point again, later.

So nowadays centuries later, following Ptolemy's brief statements, astrologers still keep the beginning point of their chart at the same place where it was in Ptolemy's time, no matter in what century or millennium they may be living. They do **not** ensure that the beginning of Aries is always moved to the point where the constellation of the Ram is located in their century! For in the tropical zodiac the sign of Aries has its fixed position, as do the other signs. They remain fixed in the model which is based on the same unchanging point where the sun's pathway crosses the Earth's equator.

So what is going on? Ptolemy was **not** affirming a zodiac based on the moving positions of the constellations. Instead his zodiac is stationary, and is based on a division of the heavens starting with the sign of Aries at the sun's location on the spring equinox. Aries is situated at the point where the sun's pathway intersects the earth's equatorial plane in March; this is the vernal sunrise point, in the northern hemisphere. By requiring the same beginning point, in the centuries after his lifetime, Ptolemy was emphasizing that the Greek tropical zodiac is going to become separated from the constellations, as they drifting backwards, so to speak.

He was revealing that this zodiac was a separate entity, not the same as the old Babylonian zodiac, nor the constellational zodiac. It is based on the intersection points on the sun's path and the equator; on the points where it turns around in its journey. Later we shall see that this is why it is called a tropical zodiac; and we shall also discover that this name is both accurate and inaccurate.

The Hellenistic Greeks already for some centuries had created a zodiac so that four of its key signs began at the equinox or solstice sunrise points; a factor which we will explore a bit later. We now need to know exactly what Ptolemy stated in his brief references to the basis of the tropical zodiac.

Claudius Ptolemy and his Tetrabiblos
In Book I, chapt.13, he writes that the sign of Aries starts at the VP (which is 21st March), and then he goes on to write from the Greek perspective about how this zodiac is associated with the yearly seasonal cycle. He describes the fixed nature of the beginning of this zodiac,

> "The beginning of the whole zodiac circle which, in its nature as a circle, can have no beginning nor end that can be ascertained; this is therefore {generally}assumed to be the Sign of Aries, which starts at the Vernal Equinox. Since the moistness of spring forms a primary beginning in the zodiac, similar to the beginning of all animal life…" (3)

This correlating of springtime to Aries in a general sort of way was a basic astrological fact in Babylonian times. Throughout the history of Babylonia, the spring equinox sun rose in front of the stars of the Ram. But the specific statement that the first degree of the sign of Aries (or 0 degrees Aries to be precise) in a tropical horoscope is actually aligned to the vernal equinox point, had already been set out by Greek astronomers long before Ptolemy. This is what is called the tropical zodiac. It is a zodiac that the Greeks made, and it is separate from the Babylonian one. The Hellenistic zodiac has four of its signs aligned precisely to the sun's yearly cycle of two solstices and two equinoxes. Whereas the Babylonian zodiac was not aligned to these points at all.

The Precession of the Equinox

One would think that if you observed where the sun rose on the same day of a month each year, it would always be the same, year in and year out. And to a casual night sky observer that is reasonably true. But actually, when viewed over centuries, the sun's position on the same day of the year moves slowly backwards, taking about 26,000 years to go right around the heavens.

This slow motion backwards is called the Precession of the Equinox (that is, the backwards movement of the equinoctial sunrise point). In fact this motion backwards is caused by a very slight wobble in the Earth's own rotating, a motion which gives us day and night. It is this motion which Hipparchus discovered (or identified mathematically).

So it is obvious in the light of the discovery of Hipparchus, that since the star background does slowly move, if the beginning point of Ptolemy's zodiac is kept in the same position, then after some centuries, this point will have a changing star background on the day when the vernal equinox occurs. (Or on any other day, if observed on the same day each for centuries.)

And because of this fact the question often arises, what is the implication of Ptolemy's statement that this new zodiac should be fixed, so its fixed beginning point would gradually cease to coincide with the changing vernal equinox constellations? That is, why does he stay with the model based on the pattern established by the sun crossing the Earth's equator at equinox times? Can we get clarity about this key point? Let's see what else he wrote.

In Chapter 26, he states that 'The beginnings of the signs are to be taken from the equinoctial and solstitial points'. Here he is affirming the Hellenistic model of aligning the zodiac to the solstices and equinoxes. (As we noted, the older Babylonian one did not have its divisions begin or end at a solstice or equinox).

And then Ptolemy goes on to emphasize that the signs or sectors of this zodiac are very real, even though they are located in a different part of space to the traditional Babylonian zodiac, or to the Constellational zodiac. The traditional Babylonian zodiac was still used by some Greek astronomers or astrologers. To explain why this zodiac must start at that special point, he writes,

> 'If another starting point were to be assumed, we would be compelled to no longer have dealings with the {actual} natures of these signs for prognostications; or {if we proceeded} we would be in error, making mistakes, transgressing and making alienated the {spiritual} powers that are operative in the zodiac sectors.' [iii]   (trans. the author)

So he is quite clear that the sectors of the tropical zodiac have an objective existence! They are not an intellectual construct. Each of the signs of this zodiac have a real objective quality. Now if we analyse these words, some interesting facts emerge. Firstly, this type of zodiac was written about by others before him; and they too insisted that this system had to be followed to achieve genuine accuracy in astrological analysis. But these two points together mean that it was not the Babylonian zodiac;

Ptolemy is arguing against this zodiac. So let's be clear, Ptolemy is not writing about the familiar Babylonian zodiac. He is writing about the Hellenistic zodiac, which the Greeks, already 600 years earlier, had aligned to the solstice and equinox. He is supporting a zodiac with its sectors or signs aligned to the sun-earth relationship. A zodiac whose signs will gradually become separated from the constellations of the sidereal zodiac. But how did it happen that this new zodiac was created? At this point we need to know more about the important zodiac of twelve segments or sectors each of the same size (thirty degrees), created by the Babylonians.

The Babylonian Equal-sized Segments zodiac
The Babylonian sidereal zodiac is made up of twelve equal-sized segments. This traditional Babylonian zodiac is based on the constellations; these star groups are simply divided up into twelve equal sectors of 30 degrees in length. (4) Each of these sectors is aligned, so far as is possible, with its constellation.

But its twelve segments or divisions are also referred to as *signs*. This of course leads to confusion for us; a sidereal zodiac which has signs! Usually the word *signs* is reserved for the tropical horoscope used in modern astrology. But, yes, the Greek word which astrologers such as Ptolemy used for a tropical horoscope's signs, (or segments), was also used by them for the divisions of the Babylonian zodiac based on the constellations! The reason this happened is that the Greek word for a zodiac sign actually just means "a one-twelfth".[iv]

Each of these one-twelfths acquired a symbol or sign to represent them graphically on a horoscope. Our modern use of the word *sign* is an incorrect use of English. When we say *zodiac sign* we actually mean, "a zodiac segment which has its own special symbol or <u>sign</u>". This Babylonian Equal-sized Segments zodiac gave their star-gazers an efficient way to carry out astronomical measurements, and to define the location of the planets over centuries of observations, see illustration 3 for a clear diagram of this.

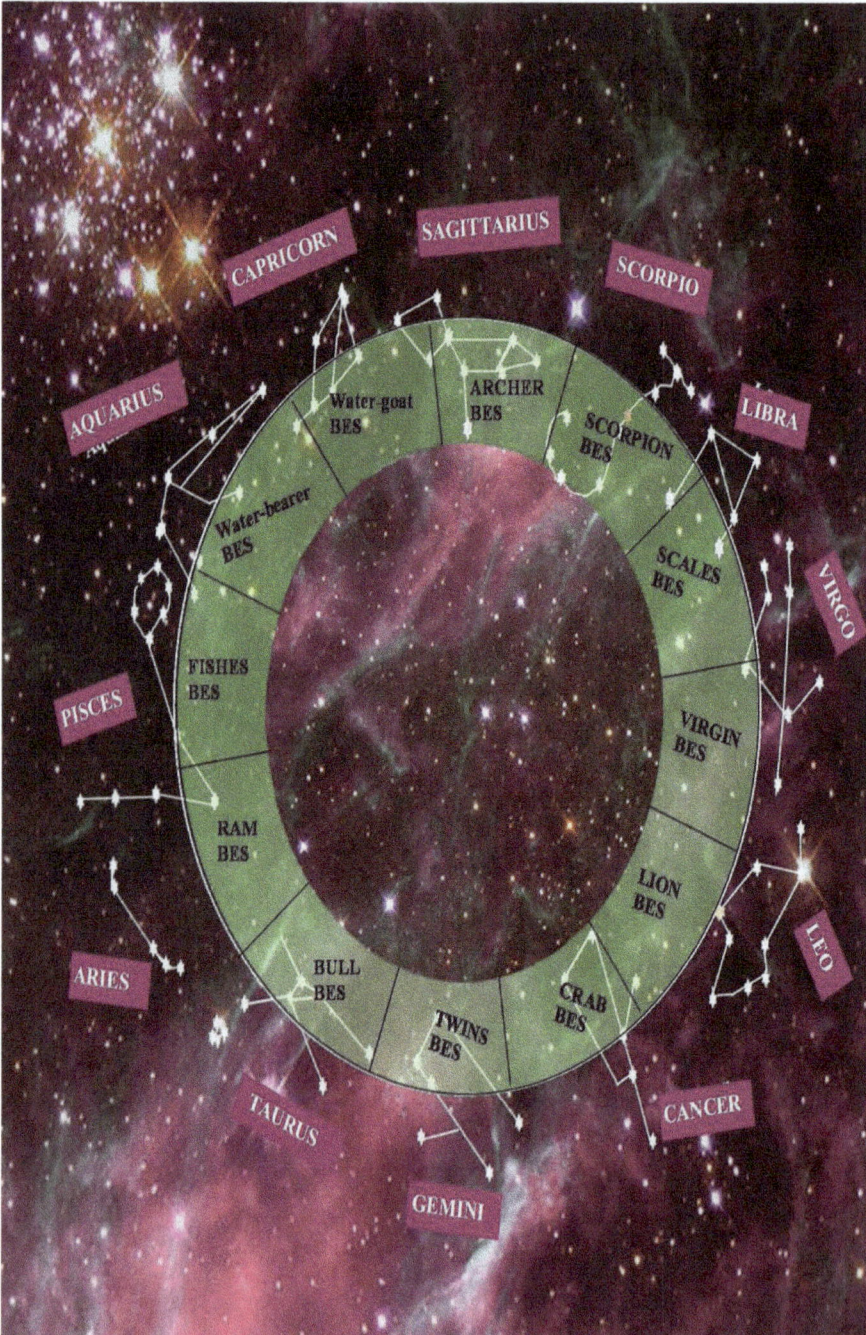

3 The Babylonian Equal-sized Segments zodiac (BES) It appears about 500 BC, its 12 segments or signs are aligned to the constellations, so far as this is possible.

A link between the Mysteries and the tropical zodiac

Some 600 years before Ptolemy, various Greek astronomers had created this zodiac which was aligned to the sun's cycle (to the solstice and equinox) so that Aries began at the vernal equinox sunrise point. For example, the astronomer Euctemon (active about 430 BC) is one person who made this intriguing change, affirming this zodiac. Unfortunately, we have no information about this man's biography at all. But we have better luck with another astronomer who also did this; namely, Callipus, who was active about 350 BC.

We know that Callipus was in fact connected to the Mysteries. The Greek Mysteries were institutions established long before these astronomers; already at the time of Homer (750BC) in many cases, or even earlier. The Mysteries were temple communities established specifically to train people in experiencing the gods, and therefore in higher thoughts and perception. The Mysteries also had the role of passing onto these students lofty secret knowledge. The people involved in them were called the Mystae. And these Mystae or priests in the Mysteries carefully guarded their knowledge about the cosmos from outsiders.

Callipus studied the stars under a man called Polemarchus, who belonged to the school of a notable teacher, Eudoxus. However, Eudoxus was a Mystae, a member of the Mysteries, as the brief details of his biography shows. As a young man Eudoxus joined the Academy of Plato, the great teacher of Hellenistic Mystery wisdom. But then, very significantly, Eudoxus left Greece after some time with Plato, to journey to the Mystery Centre of Heliopolis in Egypt.

This centre was a deeply venerated Egyptian initiatory religious centre; it was especially focussed on astronomical-astrological studies. It was to here that the sage Pythagoras and many others journeyed, over the centuries, to enter into privileged spiritual experiences and to gain access to the celestial astronomical knowledge of the Egyptians. It was also due to the priests here that the remarkable monuments on the Giza plateau were constructed. This includes the Great Sphinx which represents the sun and its associated spirit being.

And moreover Hipparchus himself, who is accredited with discovering the Precession of the Equinox, was also probably a Mystae, i.e., a student of the Mysteries. He was certainly very aware of the Mysteries and possessed what he considered to be privileged knowledge. He stated that, "the Pythagoreans kept their esoteric knowledge secret, and perhaps I should too."

So, we have evidence that the creation of a new zodiac, with its signs located in different places to that of the established Babylonian model, came from Greek astronomical researchers who either were in, or were close to, the secretive Mystery Centres of their times. Later we shall see that Ptolemy was also in the orbit of the Mysteries. Furthermore, it is very relevant here to note that the Precession of the Equinox, which takes about 26,000 years to complete, creates through this motion a kind of Great Year. This Great Year is created as the sun goes backwards through its star background over a period of about 26,000 years. (The fascinating notion of Zodiac Ages is based on this.) This well-known large cycle is correctly called the Great Year. The term Platonic Year is wrongly applied to this cycle; the Platonic Year refers to quite a different twelve-fold time cycle.

This notion of individual Zodiac Ages is affirmed in modern mystical circles, and also noted by scholars in ancient history as an underlying idea in ancient cultures. But the intriguing fact is that this large cosmic cycle is first mentioned, as a named fact, in an initiatory Hellenistic book! That is, a book that came from knowledge and experience gained in the Mysteries by a Mystae. The book is called *The Dream of Scipio*, and it was written about 50 BC by a member of the Mysteries. (5) The author was the famous Roman philosopher and statesman, Marcus Cicero. He was initiated in the Mysteries of Eleusis.[v]

This extraordinary document, put in the form of an out-of-body experience, reveals various beliefs held by people in the Mysteries with regard to the cosmos. It indicates that the ancients learnt about the Precession of the Equinox and the various zodiacs from their spiritual experiences, not from the mathematical research of brilliant men like Hipparchus. In this book by Cicero, the Earth is specifically described as a globe swirling through space, amongst other round planets! It was not a flat rectangular surface, suspended in the centre of the universe, as it was for most Hellenistic people, and as it also was during the Dark Ages. Cicero provides intriguing evidence for the existence of special knowledge about the cosmos being held in the Mysteries. Amongst this knowledge was awareness of the tropical zodiac, and knowledge of the Great Year. And Cicero also describes the round Earth as having a hot equatorial zone, and also ice-covered south and north poles![vi]

Now Ptolemy reminded his readers that the sign of Aries **starts on March 21st** (the VP); this is true of the Hellenistic zodiac. But like Hipparchus, and no doubt others, Ptolemy also knew that the constellations gradually drifts away from the fixed tropical VP. And this means that to Ptolemy although the two zodiacs were somewhat aligned in his lifetime, they would be separating off from each other. So, Ptolemy was proclaiming a zodiac that had its twelve sectors or signs quite separate from the Babylonian zodiac and also from the constellational zodiac. He is emphasizing a kind of zodiac which has its sectors based on the intersection points of the sun and the earth. And he was also teaching that these will gradually be **in a different part of space to the Babylonian zodiac**.

The Hellenistic zodiac starts with Aries, with the beginning of Aries precisely aligned to **the vernal equinox point**. But Hipparchus pointed out that this point is gradually moving! **So, Ptolemy is really talking about a second zodiac!** He is confirming that the Hellenistic tropical zodiac is in effect a second zodiac, and not just in the sense of an intellectual construct, it is a very real, actual zodiac, even if it is invisible.

Historically in ancient Babylonia, the sun had always entered the Babylonian sign of Aries (or the Hired Man as they called it) during the springtime. But the signs of this Babylonian zodiac did not have their position changed by any kind of motion. And their sign of Aries actually started a long way back from the spring equinox point.[vii]

So now the next question is, how many Greek astrologers shared Ptolemy's view that the Hellenistic zodiac had its own fixed beginning point, derived from the pattern based on the sun's path around the earth, and ignore the changing star background? Well, there are virtually no historical documents that answer this question. Some Greek astronomers or astrologers who were in agreement with Ptolemy, factored in the gradual drifting apart, and used the stationary tropical zodiac. But if they did not think about it, or could not figure out the complex motions involved, then they would have concluded that their zodiac was slowly moving; and therefore it would stay in alignment with the constellations.

But here we meet a very important point. Awareness that the tropical zodiac was separate from the traditional BES zodiac, and would no longer be aligned to the constellations was clearly known in the Mysteries, for many centuries before Ptolemy. But before we explore this, we need to be clearer about the terms, tropical and sidereal.

A tropical zodiac in some ways
Let's now go back to the question, just what are the zodiac signs, how can they be viewed as valid? If a horoscope is to be drawn up today, using the position of the planets in the constellations, it is called a sidereal horoscope, because then the positions of the planets in the star constellations are its basis, not the zodiac signs. (Sidereal comes from the Latin word for *of the stars*.) And for many people it seems so logical to use the visible Constellations Zodiac. However, almost no professional Western consultant, aiming at an accurate psychological

profiling of a person does that, for good reasons which we will explore a bit later. A chart for the same person done according to the normal tropical zodiac signs is very different to a chart done using the sidereal zodiac. Very different personality qualities are indicated.

When a horoscope is drawn up using the position of the planets in the zodiac signs, which are not in the same space as the constellations, it is called a tropical horoscope. The positions of the planets in these zodiac signs are the basis of it. These zodiac signs are said to belong to a kind of zodiac known as a tropical zodiac. But why is it called tropical? We have examined this term already, and we have seen that from the view of a zodiac based on the sun-earth intersection, it is a valid term.

We have explored the tropical system as such, but now we have to ask, is this word *tropical* fully right for the zodiac used in one's horoscope? Sure, it is tropical in terms of having its signs aligned to the points where the sun's motion intersects the Earth's equatorial plane at spring and autumn. But the term tropical also implies that this zodiac is *seasonal*. Is the zodiac used in the horoscope really seasonal?

What do the seasons have to do with one's horoscope? Two horoscopes can be drawn up for two different people having the same birthday, say December 25th. But if one is born in New York, where it is the wintertime there, and the other is born in Capetown, where it is the summertime, the seasonal aspect has no relevance at all. So the sign of Capricorn is, in itself, neither a summer nor a winter entity. The structure of the tropical zodiac is based on the sun's journey to the tropic of Cancer and the tropic of Capricorn, with the sector of Aries marked out from the point where the sun reaches the spring equinox. But this zodiac is not seasonal itself. It is global; it confers the same qualities upon a person born in one of its signs, regardless of whether they live in either northern or the southern hemisphere.

The reason that it is called a tropical zodiac goes back to the language used in Hellenistic times (ca. 350 BC - 100 AD). The locations of the signs or divisions of this zodiac were determined by the solstitial and equinoctial places of the sunrise during the year. And the Greek word translated as *tropical* actually meant to the Greeks, solstitial or equinoctial. That is, the point where the sun begins to turn back on its own course, after the summer and winter solstices, or the spring and autumn equinox. And since this zodiac begins on the spring equinox, and is aligned to the intersection of the equator by the sun's pathway, people naturally began to say that this zodiac was tropical. And in terms of this unchanging process of the sun's motion around the earth, it is indeed tropical.

But as we saw above, due to Ptolemy's works, the personal horoscope always retains, as the place where the sign of Aries begins, a certain unchanging point. So therefore, this kind of zodiac is precisely **not tropical, if by tropical one means seasonal**! For this zodiac is no longer aligned to the stars observed at the sunrise point on the spring equinox in Ptolemy's time. The springtime in the northern hemisphere now occurs when the sun is amongst the stars of the Fishes. The sign of Aries in this zodiac is not placed where the stars of Aries are to be seen.

And it is this inconsistency that irritates astronomers today, and disconcerts siderealist astrologers. Sure, it was once long ago in the Hellenistic era, but not anymore. So the term tropical – from this point of view – is incorrect. For all the associations the ancient people made about the stars of Aries with the springtime (of the northern hemisphere) and other star groups with summer, autumn and winter are now wrong.

So how did this new zodiac get so precisely associated with the sun's journey through **the seasons**? It has a natural link to the sun's movements around the year, but it does not have any such link to the seasons. Hellenistic people mistakenly thought that, since this zodiac is aligned to the equinox and solstice points, it must be inherently linked to the seasonal cycle. And this was a natural suggestion because the link between the weather of the seasonal cycle and the old BES zodiac was well-known. And with the Greeks aligning the zodiac signs to the solstices and equinoxes, their zodiac also appeared to be aligned to the seasonal weather. So some writers carried over this traditional body of knowledge about the seasonal qualities coming from the constellations to the new zodiac, naturally without factoring in the two hemispheres of our planet.

The seasons and the zodiac

The Babylonians in their BES zodiac did relate the seasonal cycle with its different weather and qualities of moist, hot, cold or dry, to their zodiac divisions or signs. But they did not start nor end their zodiac signs based on the precise position of where the sun rose on the spring equinox (or on the winter solstice.) But Ptolemy and other Greeks with access to the Mysteries, did exactly this. But as we shall see, they were working with a zodiac that transcends the weather pattern of a hemisphere. It arose from various Greek researchers who were associated with the Mysteries. So we can conclude that this new zodiac was revealed to these researchers by the leaders of the Mystery Schools. These researchers gradually worked out the mathematical and observational evidence for this new zodiac.

But when Ptolemy himself relates seasonal qualities to the zodiac, this creates an intriguing question. Just consider what we noted earlier, that after some centuries all the weather qualities assigned to the stars of the Ram by the Greeks **will no longer apply!**

It will still apply to the tropical sign of Aries, since that is part of the fixed zodiac, but of course only for the northern hemisphere. So globally the tropical signs too, are not seasonal at all. Let's get clearer about this.

33

The twelve constellations will no longer be lined up to the months and their weather qualities, as centuries pass by. So the Ram will no longer be where the spring equinox occurs. And Ptolemy, as a student of Hipparchus' works, knew that fact well! The starry background would separate from his zodiac.

So why did he link the Hellenistic zodiac signs to the seasons? The answer is, that **he did not do that**! Most of Ptolemy's comments, about the signs being linked to the seasons, are **in reference to the older Babylonian BES zodiac**, which is based on the zodiacal stars. His comments about this link are found in Chapter 9 of his Tetrabiblos. For Ptolemy worked with both zodiacs; the Hellenistic one and the old traditional BES one. His Almagest is a great and accomplished book about the stars and their positions on the celestial sphere of the heavens.

The Hellenistic zodiac is not of course really linked to the seasons. If the new zodiac were to be truly connected to the yearly seasonal cycle, it would only be relevant to the northern hemisphere! The Greek references to the seasonal influence of the stars were absorbed from the older Babylonian astronomy; but it mainly applied to the Babylonian zodiac. For in Mesopotamia, star-gazers had noted an association between the constellations of the zodiac and the weather.

Ptolemy affirmed and used the fixed sphere of the stars, so he was aware of both zodiacs. And when he gives a presentation of the qualities of the zodiac signs and mentions the visible stars in these signs,[viii] he is talking of the actual BES zodiac, with it equal-sized signs or segments. He describes what kind of elemental qualities they have; whether cool, windy, moist, dry, turbulent, etc. These elemental qualities and how they influence the natural world, are very relevant to the life-processes in nature. These associations of stars to the weather are indeed relevant, but not in regard to specific seasons; in regard to the days in which the moon is placed in them, for example. These dynamics are vital to farming that uses the influences of the planets and the moon amongst the stars, such as bio-dynamic farming.

Finally, what about Ptolemy's very brief suggestion that this weather link also applies to the Hellenistic zodiac? Well this was the product of a rather limited viewpoint, for it is only true of the one hemisphere. And when Ptolemy was living, the tropical zodiac was in alignment with the traditional zodiac and with the corresponding seasons, and so such an idea could come to mind.

The BES zodiac and the Hellenistic tropical zodiac were still closely aligned back in the Hellenistic Age. As illustration 4 shows, the start of the division of Aries in the old traditional zodiac (the BES of the Ram) was at almost the same place as the beginning of Aries in Ptolemy's Hellenistic zodiac.

4   140 AD The position of the vernal equinox sunrise point (VP) at Ptolemy's time, in relation to the several Zodiacs.

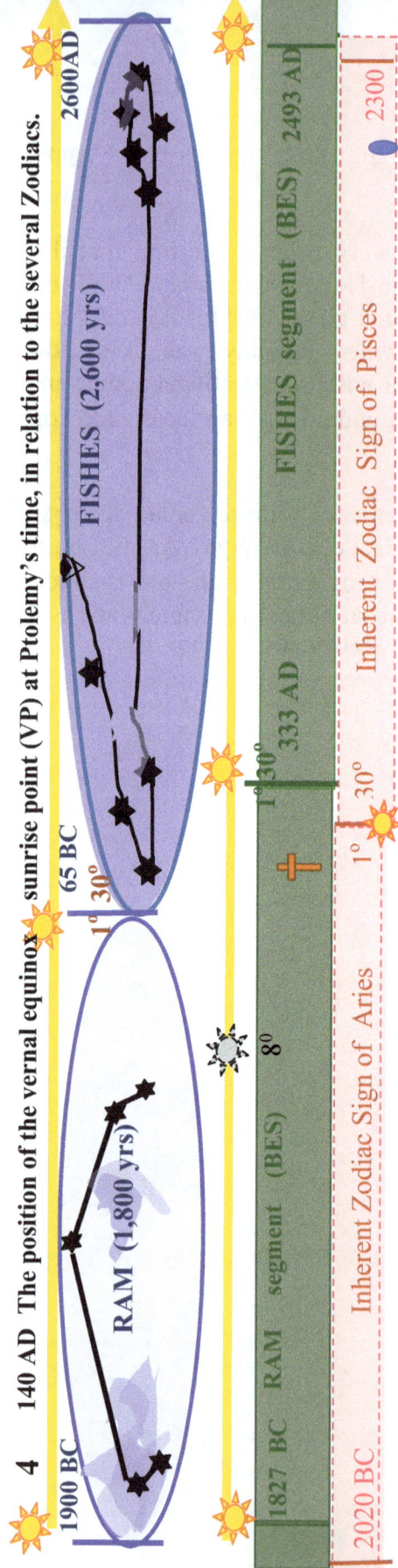

2600AD

FISHES (2,600 yrs)

65 BC

1900 BC

RAM (1,800 yrs)

140 AD

1° 30°

1° 30°

333 AD

1827 BC   RAM   segment   (BES)   8°

FISHES segment (BES)   2493 AD

Inherent Zodiac Sign of Aries

Inherent Zodiac Sign of Pisces

2020 BC

2300

30°

1°

140

8°

= 21st century

The VP sun was here = 8° in BES Aries, about 400 BC & left uncorrected by many astrologers

The coinciding of the constellations and the 'signs'.

The BES (Babylonian Equal-sized Segments) zodiac & the Constellations Zodiac do not move; they remain in a constant unchanging relation to each other. But the Hellenistic Inherent Zodiac drifts of out of alignment with both of these. So, there was an alignment of the Inherent Zodiac with the both of these at the time of Christ. However the VP (vernal equinox sunrise point) also moves slowly backwards, seen against the Constellations zodiac, the BES zodiac and the Cultural Ages zodiac, so away from where it was in Ptolemy's time.

= Inherent Zodiac (Ptolemy, etc): Only 2 signs shown, as this zodiac is **not** used to date the flow of time, but in 140 AD it is almost in the same position as the BES zodiac.

140 AD. The spring equinox point (VP) was then at:
1° in the Sign of Aries of Ptolemy's Inherent Zodiac
ca. 2° in the BES of The Ram (= "Babylonian sign of Aries")
ca. 27° in the Constellation of The Fishes

Technical note: the dates for the BES zodiac eras are based on variation of the SVP data in the Fagan-Bradley model (taken from R. Steiner)

However, a number of astrologers who drew up charts in the era of Ptolemy were not aware of the difference between these zodiacs. So it is difficult to know which zodiac they were using for their charts. Because the two zodiacs are moving apart, the name tropical (i.e. solstitial and equinoctial) as we understand this word in seasonal terms is misleading. Ptolemy himself never used this name for it. Although this zodiac is tropical in terms of one viewpoint (the sun-earth relationship), it is unfortunate that the term tropical is used, and we are going to suggest a new name, because the zodiac with the twelve signs used in a horoscope has nothing to do with the seasons at all.

It is incorrect to define the tropical zodiac as a seasonally attuned zodiac, linked with the cycle of the year. For this would absurdly also mean that it can only be used for the horoscopes of people born in the northern hemisphere. This view in effect dismisses the tropical zodiac as an intellectual fancy, but every professional counsellor using the Hellenistic zodiac to help their clients, knows that this is wrong. The accuracy of the tropical chart for people of both hemispheres can be demonstrated very effectively indeed.

The Vernal Point in Hellenistic astrology

Various astrologers in Ptolemy's time said that the point in the heavens where the sun rose on the spring equinox was either 8 or 10 degrees into the division (or sign) of the Ram in the BES zodiac.[ix] But in fact at that time, it was much nearer to the beginning of the BES sign of the Ram, (actually at 2 degrees), as diagram 3 shows. The astrologers or astronomers who believed it was still located at 8 or 10 degrees in Aries were out of date. They were only noting where the point once was, according to the old data that they inherited from the Babylonians. They were in fact unaware that this position, which was true some three or four centuries earlier, had changed; this point had moved. It does slowly drift backwards. This is precisely what Hipparchus pointed out, about 150 BC. And because of the works of Hipparchus quite a number of astrologers or astronomers did realize that in the time of

Ptolemy the sunrise point was quite near the boundary of Aries and Pisces (and not back about 10 degrees before this). This is a fact that Marcus Manilius, the 1st century Roman astrologer noted, writing at about the time of Christ.[x]

Now astronomers today make indignant attacks on astrologers for not moving this beginning point of Aries, because the sun's position against the background of the night sky slowly changes over time, about one degree every 72 years. So it now rises at a different point amongst the constellations to where it was in the time of Claudius Ptolemy. But to leave the horoscope unchanged, with the first degree of Aries aligned to the same point on the horizon where it was in the time of Ptolemy **is exactly the right thing to do, as we shall soon see.**

But this attitude of astrologers, that the beginning of the sign of Aries should remain where it was in Ptolemy's time, has been puzzling to many people when they become aware that the sun's position actually does change, when seen again on the same day of the year over centuries. People have thought that since this motion is taking place, then so too, the horoscope zodiac should be updated. In other words the beginning of the horoscope, the zero point of Aries, should be moved along, to be aligned to where the constellation of Aries is seen. Earlier we said that this is wrong. But why? **Because, as Ptolemy indicates, the tropical zodiac is an objective reality, and its signs of sectors identify the areas where the qualities of the different star constellation are to be found.** But more of that later, we still need a bit more information.

In the Babylonian Equal-sized Segments zodiac (BES), each segment tends to be aligned with its constellation. So it has its centre in the middle of the visible constellation. And in the sign of The Bull (known later as Taurus) there is a prominent star called Aldebaran at its centre, and in The Scorpion, on the opposite side of the sky, the prominent star Antares is central to the segment based on the Scorpion. The zodiac based on this system of segments is neither the zodiac of the modern horoscope, nor of the irregular astronomical constellations.

We have noted earlier that the segments or signs of the tropical zodiac of the Greeks, including Ptolemy, carry the names of the zodiac constellations, yet they are now located in quite separate places in space to that of the constellations. That the zodiac signs are not aligned to the constellations is a very major point of confusion.

They therefore appear in fact to constitute a separate zodiac. It appears to be a separate circle of 12 sectors, with its own objective existence. But if this is so, where does it exist; where is it? Let's just repeat that the starting point of the tropical horoscope, the beginning of the division or sign of Aries, is always at a certain fixed point in space. And this point is where the sun rises on the spring equinox of the northern hemisphere.

So when astrologers cast a horoscope, the beginning of the sign of Aries always remains in the same place, relative to the heavens. It is as if the apparent slow motion backwards of the stars is just being ignored. But now, after all we have noted we can say: **and it should be ignored, if this zodiac is a separate, independent thing.** Its vernal point is based on the unchanging relationship of the sun's motion to the earth's equatorial plane. One feels that there is some definite, objective entity implied by this.

But still it is not surprising that one argument against astrology and its zodiac signs is that, whereas the constellations are very real and visible, these zodiac signs are just a foolish invention of Hellenistic astrologers.[xi] These critics say if these zodiac signs or sectors aren't in the same part of space as their constellations, then really, they are just meaningless, and can have no real existence.

The inner link between the signs and constellations

It is also said by critics of astrology that it is very unfortunate that the Hellenistic astrologers gave the names of the Babylonian constellations to these apparently corresponding, but really "non-existent", zodiac signs. And so consequently, some Western astrologers have advocated creating horoscopes based on the sidereal model, where the positions of the planets in the constellations are shown.

Yet if one does that, the client will get, in the opinion of most astrologers, an inaccurate profile of their personality. But when the chart is drawn up, using these <u>apparently</u> non-existent zodiac signs, then the client gets an invaluable, deeply accurate profile of their personality! This fact shows that it is very fortunate, and very wise, that the Hellenistic astrologers gave the names of the constellations to the corresponding zodiac signs.

They did this because –

they knew that these 12 sectors, these zodiac signs, out in space around our planet, carry within them the qualities of the <u>corresponding</u> zodiac constellations!

Whoever gave the same name to the Signs as those of the Constellations, **knew exactly what they were doing!** For these were people who were drawing on the special knowledge held in the Mysteries.

It is entirely valid to associate a zodiac sign in the Hellenistic zodiac with a zodiac constellation. For these 12 sectors or segments of the zodiac used in the horoscope, which we call signs, **actually carry the same qualities as the constellations that they are named after!** The signs unfailingly bestow these relevant qualities upon each new-born baby. The **sign of Aries** carries the same quality as the stars of the **constellation the Ram**.

The **sign of Gemini** carries the same quality as the stars of the **constellation The Twins,** and so on.[xii] So the sectors in space we call the zodiac signs are the vessels of the corresponding constellations.

But how is it possible for the tropical zodiac used in a horoscope to be really connected to the zodiac constellations, since the signs are not in the same part of space as the constellations? Is it **because these zodiac signs exist in their own right, as a kind of zodiac energy field, around the Earth's upper atmosphere?** Let's see if the authorities who created astrology can tell us.

CHAPTER THREE

Who originated this zodiac system?

Where did this knowledge come from, of the invisible twelve zodiac signs and where they are located invisibly in space? And where did the knowledge of their inner link to the visible constellations come from? This zodiac, separate from the Babylonian BES zodiac, and slowly separating off from the constellations, was strongly emphasized in the writings of Ptolemy. But awareness of a separate zodiac, regarded as located near to the Earth, existed long before Ptolemy.

This understanding of the cosmos that includes a second, separate zodiac, actually came from the highest source of knowledge available to the ancient world; namely the priests of The Mysteries of their respective culture, whether Greek, Hebrew, or Babylonian. These people were the leading authorities in spiritual realities and celestial dynamics. But we need to be very aware that the knowledge about, or discovery of, this separate zodiac should not be confused with the knowledge about, or discovery of, the Precession of the Equinox. They are two separate themes, separate realities, although somewhat connected. The discovery of the separate zodiac is one thing; the discovery of the Precession of the Equinox is another thing.

The discovery of the Precession of the Equinox is reasonably attributed to Hipparchus. It is true that only from the Hellenistic Greeks, such as Aristarchus and Hipparchus does one find the astronomical-mathematical research and calculations that enable the Precession to be discovered, as a scientific fact. But it was actually not from these astronomers that knowledge of the separate kind of zodiac which Ptolemy introduced, derives.

It is important to realize that the discovery (or re-discovery) of the Precession of the Equinox does not mean that Hipparchus discovered this new separate zodiac. Nor does it mean that Ptolemy made his discovery that the zodiac is a separate thing to the BES zodiac, because of this research of Hipparchus. For Greek astronomers or astrologers, drawing on esoteric knowledge, had already created a zodiac which was a tropical zodiac. But they did not mention publicly the matter of how such a zodiac, aligned to the solstices and equinoxes, has to gradually become separated from the background constellations.

They probably were quite clear about the implications, but such knowledge was under the taboo of the Mysteries. We don't know just how the view of the universe changed for the normal Greeks, that is, those not involved in the Mysteries, once the discovery by Hipparchus became known.

But it appears that some people now thought of the celestial sphere of the heavens (or part of it) as slowly rotating, and yet they also knew that there was an immoveable firmament out there, too. The discovery of this Precession, showing the spring equinox occurring against a slowly changing background of stars, is one thing. But the existence of a new zodiac, becoming separated gradually from the Babylonian Equal-sized Segments zodiac or BES, but which is also **closely linked to the Earth**, is another thing altogether.

The fact that it had been discovered that the sunrise point of the spring equinox slowly moves across the stars, does not mean necessarily that the normal Greek astronomers concluded that their BES zodiac was moving, nor that they realized that there was another zodiac out there! In fact few would have thought of the BES zodiac as moving, for to them the zodiac was apparently a major part of the huge celestial sphere itself; of the universe. And to the people who still used the BES zodiac sunrise point, the solar cycle in general was not so important. The discovery made by Hipparchus created riddles for them. And huge riddles for us today, since we have less feeling for subtle energies than the ancients had.

Ptolemy emphasized the existence of a separate zodiac, the beginning of which (0 degrees Aries) is located at the point where the sun is seen on the spring equinox. In earlier centuries Greeks who were involved with the Mysteries knew of this zodiac aligned to the solstices and equinoxes. **But awareness of this new separate zodiac had existed already with other people, people who were the leaders of the Mysteries.**

Astrology as a part of The Mysteries
Ancient texts actually still exist today which show that awareness of the zodiac signs comes ultimately from people who were given special knowledge, special insight, through their involvement in the ancient Mysteries. Some ancient Mesopotamian clay tablets are still in existence, and there are also some Hellenistic Greek papyrus texts, in which the author expressly forbids his students from revealing the contents of these teachings!

The students were forbidden to reveal it because the knowledge was imparted to those admitted to the inner sanctum of Mystery knowledge. So it is not surprising to find that the zodiac signs are affirmed in those special writings which one could call initiatory writings. These are writings that derive from initiation experiences of acolytes in the old Mysteries.

Prof. Rochberg gives an example from long ago in the Babylonian culture, where the student is strictly ordered to keep the information secret. The version given here has been simplified for easier reading; see the Appendix for the original detailed version.

> **On eclipses of the moon.**
> Tablet of Anu-bel-sunu, lamentation priest of Anu, son of Nidintu-Anu, descendant of
> Sin-leqi-unninni of Uruk.
> Hand of Anu-aba-utêr, his son,
> scribe of Enuma Anu Enlil of Uruk.
> Uruk, month I, year 12.

Antiochus III (The Great) and Antiochus, his son, were kings.

Whoever reveres Anu and Antu will not remove the tablet in an act of thievery.
It is a Computational Table.
Wisdom of the highest order,
exclusive knowledge concerning heaven and earth, a secret of the scribal masters.
An expert may show (it) to another expert.
A non-expert may not see it. It is a restriction
of Anu, Enlil and Ea, the great gods. (6)

This is a clear indication of how astronomical-astrological knowledge of the cosmos was guarded from popular exposure. And furthermore, there is the example of a Hellenistic astrologer called Vettius Valens, who strictly required that his readers take an oath to guard his words, **because they should treat them as being <u>of the Mysteries</u>.** (!)[xiii]

This passage is translated in an English version as, "to guard his words as a mystic secret." But the word mystic is not quite right culturally, for we need to differentiate between a mystic (such as Teresa of Avila) and the Mystae of the pre-Christian Mysteries. Western cultures are familiar with individual mystics in the Christian era. This is someone who is subject to spontaneous and not always uplifting psychic experiences.

But as noted above, the mystae are in another class; they were trained and educated in old and venerated institutions dedicated to spiritual knowledge. So Vettius is saying, when more exactly translated, that his students should regard his teachings as something that **derives from the Mysteries**.[xiv] And another statement by Vettius confirms this fact. He says, his students "must not share this wisdom with the ignorant or **uninitiated**". (7)

No wonder that the old esoteric documents are not interested in underlined defending the tropical horoscope. They don't feel any need to do that; instead they comment on the deeper spiritual implications of this zodiac. In fact in these writings, the twelve zodiac signs are described as being a kind of second zodiac which receives and activates the qualities (soul qualities) from the corresponding star constellations. A careful examination of ancient Greek texts that are often ignored in the study of the origins of astrology, reveals some fascinating glimpses at how tropical zodiac signs were viewed as fully real and valid, by precisely those who attained to high spiritual wisdom in their own culture. Let's see what these few texts say.

The zodiac signs affirmed by the Grecian Mysteries
Several references to the actual tropical horoscope signs, are made by a fascinating Christian sage, Titus Flavius Clement of Alexandria, who wrote between 193-215 AD. It is likely that he had been initiated into a Mystery religion, before becoming a Christian. It was in his writings for example, that modern scholars of ancient Grecian culture found the secret password verse used by those who were initiated into the lofty Eleusinian Mysteries.

His Christian writings hint at deeper esoteric knowledge; in fact he taught a kind of cosmic and cosmopolitan Christianity. Clement was an authority in the Alexandrian church, and the teacher of the saintly scholar Origenes, regarded by many as eastern Christianity's greatest sage, (185-254 AD). And he is the author of a letter, which ca used an enormous uproar amongst theologians world-wide some 30 years ago, when it was found. The letter was discovered by accident, hidden inside the cover of a book, in an ancient monastery. He refers to a secret gospel written by St. Mark for the initiation of Christians, and also he makes a few brief comments about initiation procedures for Christians! This is not the place to examine the brief statements in his letter, but it is important to know about it, because then we can understand that in his books secret initiatory wisdom could faintly show through. There are three main references to the zodiac in his writings.

These references are brief, but startling. Firstly, he comments on the mention in the Bible of the mysterious sacred garment worn by the High Priest of Israel. This was a garment which has twelve jewels set in it, in four rows of three. This garment or rather, breastplate, adorned with twelve gemstones, had a pouch in it, where two small objects were kept, known as the Urim and Thummin. These two objects are described in the Bible as being used by the priests to actually ascertain the will of God. St. Clement comments on this saying that,

> 'the twelve stones, set in four rows on the breast-plate, <u>display for us the zodiac circle</u>, according to the four solstice and equinoctial points of the year.'[xv] (trans. the author) (8)

From this comment we see that to Clement, the sacred gemstone arrangements enabling the High Priest to commune with God, were actually symbols of the twelve zodiac signs of the Hellenistic zodiac! He refers to the four solstitial and equinoctial points of the year and thereby identifies the zodiac as the tropical zodiac used by Ptolemy, and not the Constellational Zodiac nor the BES zodiac.

In another place, Clement is speaking of the ancient Greek sage Plato, and he mentions an incident involving a Greek myth, set in a mythical time long before Plato. This myth is about a hero called Er, whom Plato speaks of at the end of his book *The Republic*. According to a later Greek writer called Colotes, the great sage Plato inserts a passage in this book about the ancient Persian sage Zarathustra. This passage is about the legends concerning the death of the great Persian prophet. The passage recounts the legend that says when this Persian sage died, he was resurrected after twelve days (!)

Actually this odd accusation from Colotes of such a strange passage from Plato isn't to be found in Plato's book, as we know it today. But this is what Clement says of this supposed comment,

> "Plato speaks of this incident, possibly only because of {the intriguing nature of} this resurrection of Zarathustra in 12 days. Or possibly indeed because he is hinting at how the ascending of souls (after death) occurs along the pathway of the twelve zodiac signs. The same thing, of these signs being a pathway, is also reported in regard to {the process of} being conceived, of coming into being (on the Earth)."
>
> (8) [xvi] (trans. the author)

Notice that Clement writes, the zodiac signs are reported of as being the path to incarnation. (!) Reported by whom?? Clement just does not say; but it must be the sages who were in charge of the Mysteries. Here Clement, the most mystical of ancient Christian church fathers, is fully affirming the reality of the tropical zodiac signs as a reality known in the Mysteries. He and his student Origenes were fully aware of the tropical zodiac of course, and they were aware of Ptolemy, whose teachings were published only about 60 years before Clement wrote these words. As we shall see later, Origenes makes it clear that Ptolemy's proclamation of a fixed, separate zodiac was spreading actively through the Hellenistic world. In fact already in the time of Origenes the anonymous astronomical book, *Handy Tables*, was written. This book provided Ptolemy's data in a form designed for practical use by astrologers; so they could use the tropical zodiac correctly. The tropical zodiac was alive and well already then, despite modern siderealists doubting this.

As Alexander Jones in his book *Ptolemy's First Commentator* has established, the *Handy Tables* book was already in use in the late second century. It had been wrongly ascribed to a late fourth century scholar, called Theon. Theon no doubt also used

Ptolemy's work. And that is important because Theon was the father of the spiritual teacher Hypatia, the greatest woman sage of the Hellenistic world.

Now here in these words of Clement, the fixed zodiac signs actually appear to be something that he had already known about, from confidential Mystery texts, in which there was a specific knowledge concerning this zodiac. For Clement is not speaking from a personal hunch, (nor from Christian theology!) Here the zodiac signs are integrated into the structure of the cosmos; there is a deep interlinking of the human soul with the zodiac signs. And again, we notice that this writer has no interest in defending the validity of this zodiac.

What he reveals appears to be a concept taught in the Mysteries; namely that not only are these signs valid, but that they form a kind of pathway up into the heavenly spheres. And likewise the descent down to birth is via these signs. It is in this process, he reports, that the appropriate sun-sign is determined for the soul! So, to this respected authority (as with Theon and Hypatia) the Ptolemaic zodiac signs are not fictitious nonsense, even though they are not visible.[xvii]

The zodiac signs in the Hebrew Mysteries

And now, let's see what Hebrew sages of antiquity understood the astrological zodiac of twelve signs to be, and where they are in space. Firstly, we shall note briefly the words of a deeply learned and spiritually oriented Hebrew writer, Philo Judaeus. Philo was writing in the years 30-45AD, on many spiritual and religious themes. He, like Clement, makes veiled references to initiation. And like St. Clement of Alexandria, Philo views the tropical zodiac as deeply valid, and as the basis of the Urim and Thummin breastplate of the Hebrew High Priest;

> '...the twelve stones on the breast {plate}, arranged in four rows, each of three stones. What else are these than signifiers of the circle of the zodiac? And indeed this zodiac is divided into four parts, each with three signs;

these divisions setting up the seasons of spring, summer, autumn, winter; the four turning points (solstices and equinoxes)...' (9)   [xviii]   (trans. the author)

Philo was writing this about 200 years before St. Clement wrote his works. Here we find a clear reference to the tropical zodiac as the basis of the mysterious tool for divine communion by the Hebrew sages, by a deeply learned and spiritual sage, with knowledge of the Mysteries. Philo in his writings referred to the attainment of higher consciousness, and also the need to avoid involvement in the now decadent Mystery Centres.

But more detailed knowledge which reveals the secret of the zodiac used in our horoscopes, comes from a sacred Hebrew book, the famous Book of Enoch. This book consists of various texts about seeing the cosmos on a spiritual level; it is a kind of initiatory book. The book consists of various reports of a similar kind that have been combined together. The book was compiled about 100 or 150 years before Christ. The writer adopts the name Enoch because he feels an inner spiritual link to Enoch. So the Book of Enoch is not a normal theological book. It contains revelations about spiritual realities from initiation experiences, where the writer reports on what he saw (or if you like, believes he saw) in the cosmos.

The Book of Enoch was deeply respected by great writers of the early Christian era. Various scholars have concluded that there are several dozen statements in the New Testament that can be seen as closely linked to passages found in this book. We noted earlier that the Zodiac signs **carry within them the qualities of the corresponding zodiac constellations**. And very importantly, in this Hebrew initiatory Book of Enoch we are told that these zodiac signs are a kind of zodiac template which is **located close to the Earth. So, just like Ptolemy, Enoch writes of a second zodiac!**

The book reports on a spiritual experience wherein Enoch is led up by an angel above the Earth and amongst the planets and stars. He writes of what his vision shows him, and amazingly, he reports that there are <u>two</u> zodiacs. One is the BES zodiac, and the other is another zodiac, which is much nearer to us. It is near to the Earth,

> chapter 74: For the angel Uriel showed to me the zodiac signs and the times and the years and the days, which the Lord hath set for ever over all the luminaries of the heaven....the sun, the moon and the stars, and all the ministering Beings which make their revolution in all the chariots of heaven. In like manner, Uriel showed to me twelve doors open in the circumference of the sun's chariot in the heavens], through which the rays of the sun break forth ...[probably the BES zodiac along the ecliptic].
> And also, I saw twelve portals in the heavens, **at the periphery of the Earth*** (i.e., the upper atmosphere). Out of these go forth {energies from} the sun, the moon and the stars, and all the influences of heaven in the east and in the west {towards the Earth}.
> (* lit. 'at the ends of the Earth)   (10)

In the next chapter he refers again to this more terrestrial twelve-fold zodiac,

> Chapter 75: "And **around the periphery of the Earth*** I saw twelve portals open to all the quarters of the heavens, from which the winds go forth and blow over the Earth."   (* lit. "at the ends of the Earth")

So, two zodiacs! The one that is described as high up in the cosmos is the Babylonian Equal-sized Segment zodiac (the BES). We noted earlier that this zodiac, a set of 12 equal-sized segments, was established by the Babylonians. The seers and teachers of the Hebrew people would have learnt much about this during the time of their Babylonian Captivity (about 600 BC). The second zodiac circle however, the one that Ptolemy also wrote about, is near us!

Another text from this same esoteric Hebrew tradition has survived, which is also dedicated to Enoch. It is known as the Slavonic Enoch. It was written about the time of Christ. This other text has more to add. The writer reports seeing the zodiac in his spiritual experience, up there amongst the stars, above the sphere of Saturn. But then he refers to a second, more terrestrial zodiac circle, and very importantly for us he identifies its location as near to the so-called moon sphere,

> '…these spirit beings showed me the other pathway, that of the moon, being twelve great gates.' (10)

Significantly the writer then reports on the yearly motion **of the sun** through this zodiac, a zodiac which is not so far away from our planet. He reports that the sun takes about 30 days to go through each of the twelve portals (zodiac signs). So this is not about the path of the moon; it is about the sun's journey through a zodiac. But a zodiac which is reflected as it were in an energy field, within 'the sphere of the moon'.

When something is below the orbit of the moon, it is said in such Hellenistic texts to be in the sphere of the moon. And in this area they also located the life-forces (or Ch'i) that determine the growth and fertility processes in the plant, animal and human realms of our planet. This zodiac is depicted in illustration 5, together with the BES zodiac. This illustration gives a clear view of the two zodiacs.

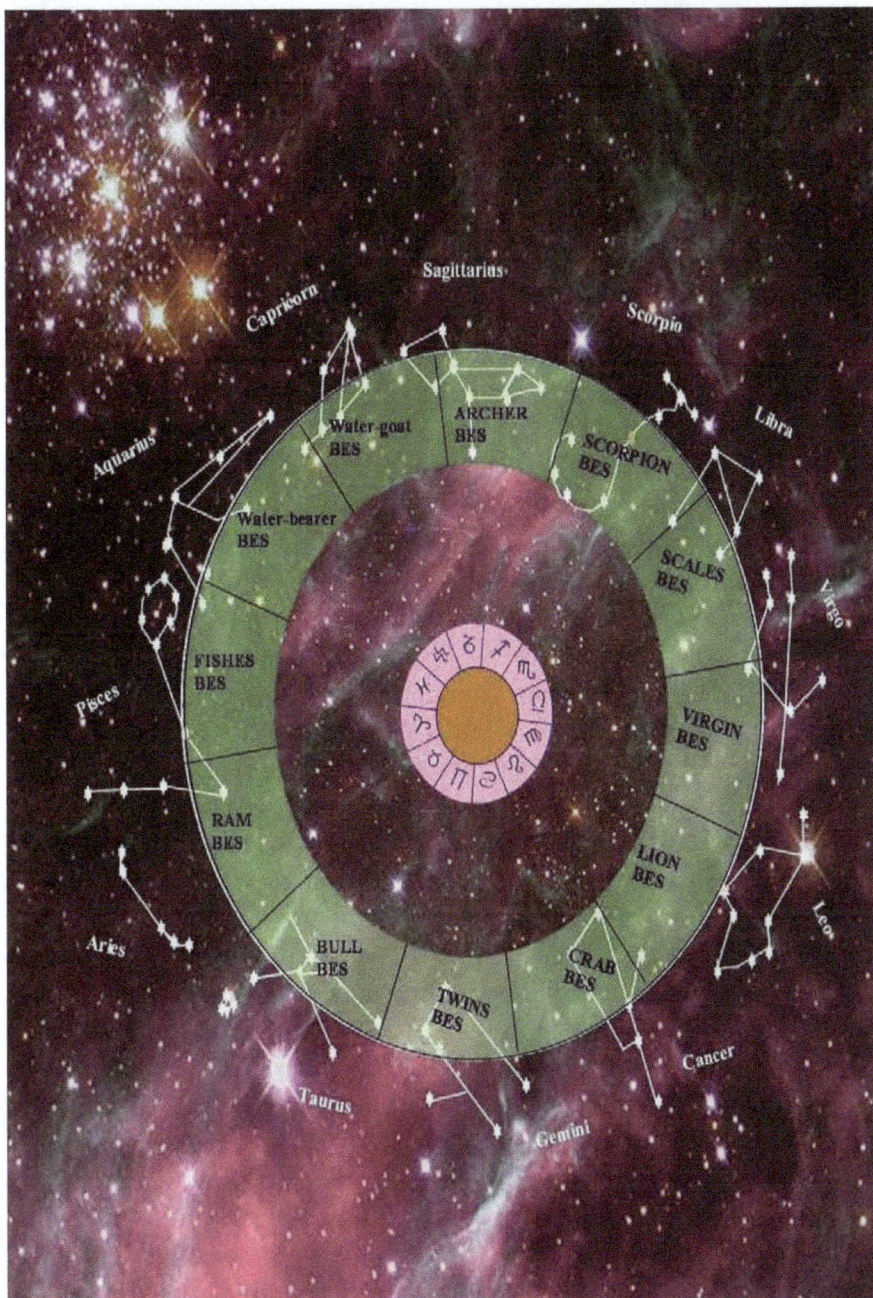

5   The Inherent Zodiac. Shown here in pink, the Inherent Zodiac envelops the Earth. This 12-fold energy-field is situated above the Earth's atmosphere. Its sectors or 'signs' each receive and activate the corresponding zodiac constellation's influences.

The answer emerges

So how can one resolve these remarkable statements into something meaningful? The zodiac of twelve signs used in a horoscope, and called a tropical zodiac, was regarded by the leaders of the great initiatory Mystery Centres, as a very real, but non-physical thing. Now we have just seen that the Book of Enoch knows about the tropical zodiac. But in fact, it is very likely that what is written in that book actually already existed for several centuries as a secret oral tradition. So, following the standard pattern for the transmission of spiritual teachings in antiquity, it was no doubt written down some centuries <u>after</u> the experiences actually occurred. And this tells us that it is very likely that the Babylonians knew of this Hellenistic zodiac, back in 600 BC, and that perhaps it was known long before that.

And in fact, this implies that it was probably known in the secret Babylonian Mystery knowledge, as well as in Hellenistic Greek and Jewish Mystery knowledge. The eminent astrological scholar, Robert Hand, has established that the Babylonians did make use of the tropical system of astrology. (11)

So, the Book of Enoch shows that the new zodiac system exists, they believed, as a field of energy situated a little beyond the planet's own biosphere; so between us and the moon. A kind of reflection of the remote starry Zodiac, but embedded in the upper reaches of an ethereal energy field surrounding the Earth. Of course, for many people today, belief in a part of the energy spectrum not yet officially discovered by science, is not an easy thing. The presence of subtle energies existing anywhere in the living ecosystem of our planet, including enveloping its thin, tenuous atmosphere may appear to some as an unusual idea. But the existence of such energies is an acceptable idea for those who accept Ch'i or prana or the idea of a life-force behind all livings things, or who respect the worldview of the ancient initiatory Mysteries.

So, summing up, the view of the ancient Mysteries was that a zodiac with 12 divisions or signs exists as an energy field around our planet, up above the atmosphere. This zodiac is a layer with 12 segments, which receives and then confers on human beings, the energy of their respective star constellation. It appears to derive its structure from the pattern established by the intersection of the earth's equator by the sun's path, (the ecliptic). And so in that specialized sense it is tropical. But this structure transcends the northern hemisphere's seasonal dynamics. The zodiac stars, (the Constellational Zodiac), and the BES zodiac are far away, in galactic space.

The spatial disjunction between the Earth's own <u>inherent</u> zodiac energy field and these stars is irrelevant. Because, the sector designated as say, Sagittarius, is receptive to the energies from the constellation of the Archer, and so on. And such a process occurs beyond the time-space continuum. It is on this ethereal level of existence that the Inherent Zodiac exists. We noted earlier that Ptolemy was in effect writing about a second zodiac. Now, in his famous book "Tetrabiblos" Ptolemy refers to just such an ethereal energy field that encompasses the Earth, as the realm from which the zodiac exerts its influence. Speaking from the holistic mind-set that held sway long ago, prior to the materialistic views of today, he says that,

> "…it is clear to everyone that a certain power, derived from the ethereal upper atmosphere, is diffused over and pervades the integument around the Earth." [xix] (trans. the author) (3)

The Greek expression translated by me here as the word *integument* refers to an atmospheric layer enveloping the planet. Ptolemy goes on to say that the elements of warmth and air below the moon are influenced by various celestial forces coming from this ethereal field. This ether or ethereal energy field in the upper atmosphere, was regarded in the Hellenistic Age as a reality; a realm from which our Ch'i or life-forces derive. [xx] This zodiac, surrounding our planet as an energy field, receptive to the influences from the constellations, we can call **the Inherent Zodiac**. This zodiac is inherent to our planet.

It is a permanent part of the Earth's outer atmosphere, so to speak.

And now that we know about the existence of this Inherent Zodiac, we can answer the question; why is it that the constellations (and the BES zodiac) are drifting apart from the (semi-tropical) Inherent Zodiac? Why are they apparently moving apart at the speed of one degree in 72 years, or the entire 360 degrees of the heavens, in 26,000 years?

They are moving apart for the very same reason that the constellations drift backwards, namely the Precession of the Equinox. The Inherent Zodiac is part of the Earth; and the Earth as we know makes a slow wobble each year, causing the spring equinox sunrise point, to appear to move slowly backwards at the speed of one degree in 72 years. This puts it back along the heavens by a small amount every year. So, viewed from the Earth, the sunrise point is slowly going backwards against the great circle of the heavens, see illustrations 6a & 6b.

And, because the Inherent Zodiac is a part of the Earth, part of its upper atmosphere so to speak, then this same wobble also causes the position of the Inherent Zodiac with its twelve signs, to move by the same distance, if you were to theoretically project it out onto the circle of the heavens. Illustration 5 shows the Precession of the Equinox clearly. You can see how over 2,160 years, the sunrise point has moved back around the circle of the heavens. Illustrations 6a & 6b show the Precession of the Equinox about every 2,000 years, but in addition they show approximately how the Inherent Zodiac is also moving backwards. You can see how the sectors (or signs) of the Inherent Zodiac are also slowly moving around the heavens.

These diagrams show how the sun appears in a different part of the heavens on the spring equinox, when seen over millennia. But also, it is shown how the Inherent Zodiac signs are precessing through the heavens, as well.

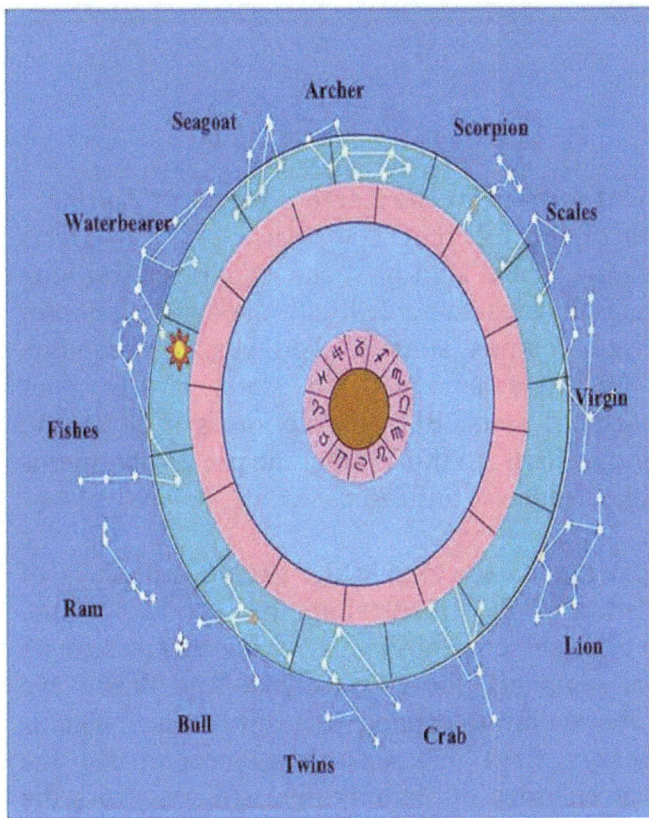

Precession of the Equinox

6A   21st Century AD

The position of the sun on March 21 in our times; it is near the end of the constellation of the Fishes

The starting point of the Inherent Zodiac (the beginning of Aries) is now at the end of the stars of the Fishes.

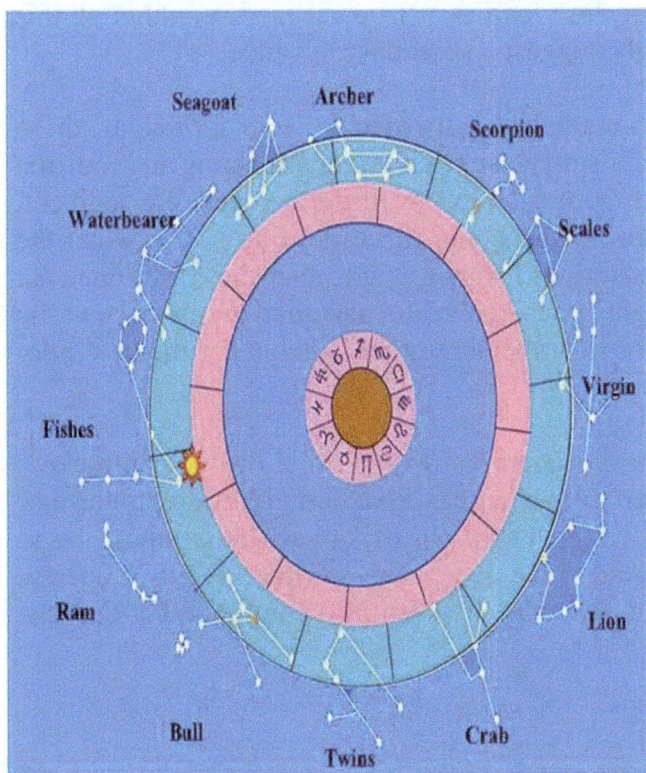

6B
1st Century AD

The sun at this time was entering the Fishes on March 21.

The starting point of the Inherent Zodiac (the beginning of Aries) was also the stars of the Fishes.

Chapter Four

Not only a tropical zodiac but the Earth's Inherent Zodiac

The zodiac signs of the Inherent Zodiac used by astrologers start at the beginning of the sign or sector of Aries. And long ago, this beginning of Aries coincided with the constellation of Aries at the spring equinox sunrise. And yes, this equinox sunrise point, out there amongst the stars, slowly goes backwards amongst the stars. But this motion is irrelevant to personal astrological charts; to think about the precession in this context is to invoke needless confusion.

Far away amongst the stars we have the twelve groupings of zodiac constellations; the Constellational Zodiac. And, secondly, we have the ancient Babylonian division of these stars into twelve equal segments, the BES zodiac. And thirdly we have, not so far above our atmosphere, the third zodiac. This is a twelve-fold energy field that acts as a receptor for the swirling, turbulent energies of stars as they stream across the vastness of the galaxy towards us. This is the Inherent Zodiac, which can also be described as a 'tropical' zodiac, although this term does wrongly suggest a seasonal relevance.

Apportioned into mathematically precise sectors, or signs, these sectors absorb the starry-astral energies streaming in from the galaxy, and hold them each in a well-defined specific segment. They enable each human being to be born at a time when the planets, the houses and rising sign, can be positioned in precisely the right place to create just that group of specific qualities that constitute the correct personality for the new-born baby.

As professional astrologers know well, one degree can make a big difference here. A planet can then be in a different house or different sign, it can just step out of, or just into, opposition to another planet. And if we accept the spiritual belief of ancient cultures, we can see why it is entirely unimportant that the tropical zodiac is not in the same place as the constellations. Since the Inherent Zodiac energy field is an integral part of our planet's life-system, it only moves backwards in the sense that it is part of the Earth, which has a slight wobble as its rotates.

The presence of a life-force field surrounding the Earth's upper atmosphere with twelve sectors, each of which resonates to one of the twelve zodiacal constellations, is an intriguing idea. An idea that was taught in ancient texts from the Mysteries. This is the origin of the Inherent Zodiac.

The wonderful phenomenon of snow-flakes is relevant here. For these give an indication of the existence of such a life-force operative in the upper atmosphere. Most larger snowflakes are shaped as a six-sided figure; it seems that the imposition of this lovely form is due the influence of an energy, like Ch'i or prana, rather than to any physical or chemical properties of frozen water.[xxi]

SNOWFLAKES

Photographs of snow flakes reveal the strange fact that most have of these have a hexagram or six-sided star shape. Indicating that they are subject to an energy, operative in the atmosphere, which is unknown to science

So summing up, the implications of the statements from these ancient texts is as follows. From twelve specific points amongst the encircling sphere of the zodiac constellations, starry energies flow out, swirling and surging. Upon approaching the Earth's upper atmosphere, these energies encounter an energy field with a geometrically precise, twelve-fold structuring. Each of these life-force sectors acts as an ethereal energy-field receptacle to its corresponding starry counterpart (or astral counterpart as the astronomers say).

So, the zodiac which is the basis of our horoscopes, is **not** a tropical zodiac in the limited hemispherical sense. (Although it is tropical in terms of its link to the sun-earth relationship.) It is not connected to the seasonal cycle, as such. It is an ethereal energy field in which the starry-astral energies of the constellations are held. And hence it is a global reality; that's why a horoscope using this zodiac can be drawn up for a person born in either hemisphere. And this creates the capacity for a horoscope to be so mathematically precise.

If for example, in a horoscope Mercury is just one degree outside the sector or sign of Taurus, and is thus in the sector named after Gemini, it then activates the qualities of Gemini (located in the corresponding constellation) in the person born at that time. Then that person will have a flexible mind-set, with quick mental responses, instead of being very steady and earth-connected as the mind would be with the Taurean position. So the twelve fold zodiac of modern astrology is an inherent zodiac, a part of the Earth's own energetic field or aura.

And now here we must note a really striking fact, a fact that has been commented on for centuries. It concerns Ptolemy's extremely important description of the zodiac as being fixed. Ptolemy actually did not loudly proclaim the remarkable fact of this Inherent Zodiac, as a fixed zodiac. He just let it be known in a very strange, understated way, that there exists this fixed tropical zodiac separate from the mobile sidereal zodiac.

Ptolemy and the Mysteries

It is obvious to the scholar, on reading the Tetrabiblos, that Ptolemy was in fact under considerable constraints as to how much to comment on the Inherent Zodiac, as a separate independent zodiac. For Ptolemy gave this information about the nature of the zodiac very briefly, without really giving a full commentary as to the huge implications of this strange feature. He was under restraints because this zodiac was known to the sages of the Mysteries.

We have already noted that knowledge of these signs, and their deep link to the human being, existed in the Mysteries. It appears that Ptolemy was very aware of the taboo about revealing these secrets of the cosmos, which had traditionally belonged to the Mysteries. Indeed it is likely that Ptolemy himself was a member of the Mysteries. For in his book Tetrabiblos, where he emphasizes the Inherent Hellenistic zodiac, he very mysteriously mentions the Mysteries. He makes an entirely unnecessary reference, but in a very respectful manner. It is in Book 2 Chap. 3 where he writes of how there are different planetary influences active in different parts of the world. He says of his own general area, Greece-Macedonia-Crete-Asia Minor, (where great Mystery Centres did exist), that "it is under the influence of Venus". He then gives this area the highest praise, commenting that the people here

> "...are in the highest degree familiar with sacred Mysteries, owing to the evening focus and dynamics of Venus."

This mysterious statement implies that the spiritual quality of Venus are accessed in the rites of the Mysteries in this area, and also that these are so spiritual that the inhabitants of that part of the world were especially blessed! It is known that the Mysteries were to some extent focused on planetary deities, however this is still a strange, veiled statement. But above all, **it is quite unnecessary**. We don't have space here to analyze the mystical implications of this strange statement, but politically it certainly shows that Ptolemy himself is either a member of the Mysteries, or that he is showing great respect here, **to avoid upsetting these institutions**; especially the Mystery sites in the area where he was living. There were very severe punishments for those who revealed the hidden Mystery knowledge; it was really taboo.

So Ptolemy wanted to encourage professional work in an astronomical-astrological way with the Inherent Zodiac, known otherwise only to those in the Mysteries. And yet he did not want to upset the authorities responsible for the Mysteries. This is the reason for his brief, curt style, and also his respectful tone with regard to the Mysteries. We saw earlier how Vettius Valens made his students take a solemn oath of secrecy about such astrological themes.

Fortunately Ptolemy could claim from the brilliant work done by earlier researchers such as Hipparchus, that in fact scientific research was now available concerning the Precession of the Equinox. This research permitted him to publicly work with this zodiac, as an associated fact of the Precession.

The Hellenistic tropical Inherent Zodiac was actively used already in the 1st century AD (and earlier); but Ptolemy's research had a substantial impact, and within half a century of Ptolemy's work, and from then on into the 4th, 5th and 6th centuries, his new zodiac, which we can call the Inherent Zodiac, became widely used. As Prof. Neugebauer has shown, horoscopes dating from several centuries after Origenes have been preserved, horoscopes which are based on Ptolemy's tropical system. (12). I have constructed some of these horoscopes, using the dates given in these old documents, using modern computer software (the excellent Halloran AstroDelux system). This shows clearly that these horoscopes are tropical. The positions of the planets in the printed horoscope using 21st century software, are either identical, or very nearly identical, to what these early horoscopes stipulate (from the 1st to the 5th centuries).

Chapter Five

The Inherent Zodiac 100-500 AD

We have already noted that in AD 30-40 Philo wrote about the Hellenistic zodiac, confirming its validity. And Clement of Alexandria likewise wrote about them in the late second century. It is interesting to note that in the writings of a great Christian sage, we can find a valuable testimony to the thriving interest in Ptolemy's Inherent Zodiac, already in the third century AD.

This writer is the famous Christian scholar, Origenes of Alexandria, a man who is often placed on the level of St. Augustine and St. Aquinas. He wrote his main works about one century after Ptolemy, between 230 and 250 AD. In a commentary on the Book of Genesis, placed in the famous *Philocalia*, an anthology of his writings, Origenes is writing against the fatalistic way that popular astrologers claimed to be able to divine the future.

The passage of interest to us here occurs in a long section opposing the fatalism implied in the divination technique (auguries) used by the Hellenistic astrologers. Origenes was not writing against psychological analysis via this new kind of horoscope, which was anyway only in a primitive stage in those days. This passage says as follows,

> "The theorem is often put forward, showing that the zodiac circle moves in a similar way to the planets, going from west to east at the rate of one part in 100 years; and that this motion, over much time, changes and crosses-over the position of the zodiac signs {relative to the visible zodiac}. So there happens to be, on the one hand, the **mentally-discerned** zodiac signs, and on the other hand, as it were, the **shape** {the

perceptible constellations} of these signs." [xxii]

(author's trans.)   (13)

It is interesting to note that the verb used by Origenes about the drifting apart of the BES and the Inherent Zodiac, means both to change and to cross-over. And both of these together describe precisely the actual process that really happens as the Inherent Zodiac and the constellations drift apart. The signs cross-over the constellations (and the BES zodiac) and change their position. So here Origenes is providing further evidence for the widespread interest in this work of Ptolemy, based on the Hellenistic Inherent Zodiac that is drifting apart from the constellations (and the BES zodiac), through a motion in some way due to the Precession of the Equinox. Origenes calls the Inherent Zodiac a mentally-discerned zodiac; and contrasts it to the sense-perceptible zodiac.[xxiii]

And yet sometimes the argument is put forward that there are no references to the tropical zodiac in Ptolemy's work; that Ptolemy did not actually intend to set up a new, separated kind of zodiac! And it may even be said that most astrologers in the Hellenistic world, and for centuries later, kept on using the standard BES system, ignoring Ptolemy. This is incorrect. For the above words from Origenes, perhaps not well known in astrological circles, show that the separated Hellenistic zodiac emphasized by Ptolemy was actively used and widely debated. However it is also true that there is evidence of astrologers who were unaware of or ignored Ptolemy in these same times.

As a thorough examination of the evidence shows, the Inherent Zodiac was a deeply respected and widely used zodiac in the Hellenistic Age and on into later Byzantine Ages. In early medieval times the use of this Inherent Zodiac in the Hellenistic world spread to the European mainland, and also to the Arabian world.

Despite church disapproval of some aspects of astrology as Origenes shows here, astrology did continue on in Christendom.

In the Renaissance it underwent a major revival, but it also became the springboard for the development of astronomy. This new science, as it took on the skeletal materialistic viewpoint of the modern times, gradually pushed astrology out of the respected halls of academia.

The over-all context of Ptolemy's new zodiac can be seen in illustration 4. Above are the constellations of the Ram and the Fishes, below these in green are the corresponding BES of the Ram and the Fishes. And below the green BES zodiac are the pink blocks of the Inherent Zodiac. Actually these play no part in the flow of time, so they are shown here only to make clear how there was an alignment of the Inherent Zodiac and the BES in the first century AD.

However, to fully realize that this zodiac is a reality, one needs to know about the remarkable accuracy of the horoscope used in psychological profiling. For those who are aware of the remarkable work done over the last 50 years in this regard by insightful and intelligent practitioners, it is quite clear that such a mechanism as this Inherent Zodiac exists.

The work of Robert Hand is a valuable example of the accuracy and depth of understanding of the human personality that astrology can provide. The works of Martin Schulman in regard to the Lunar Nodes,[xxiv] and Jeanne Avery in regard to the Rising Sign are other notable examples. Such people as these, and many others, have taken further the pioneering work done by 19th and 20th century astrologers (often Theosophists), and through extensive case studies, have developed an invaluable tool for professional psychological profiling.

Conclusion

It's been quite a journey! We have seen that the kind of questions posed in popular debate just didn't allow the answers to emerge. So what have we discovered in this exploration of the zodiac signs?

* We have seen that there are several zodiacs.

Firstly, there is the visible Constellational Zodiac of the star groups through which the sun passes on its journey around the heavens (the ecliptic).

The second is the Babylonian division of the constellations into twelve equal-sized segments; the BES zodiac.

The third zodiac is **the Inherent Zodiac**, which is a reflection of the BES zodiac, and exists as an energy-field, located around the upper atmosphere of the Earth. It is this zodiac which is used to create the natal horoscope. The intersection of the sun's path to the earth's equatorial plane, considered as a global dynamic, form the outline of this zodiac.

* According to ancient Hebrew mystics, the Inherent Zodiac exists above the atmosphere, as an energy-field.

* The Inherent Zodiac's precise sectors or signs makes possible the precise positioning of planets and Houses and the Zenith and Rising sign and Lunar nodes, etc. All of these create (or rather make dynamically manifest) the personality of the new-born person.

* The Inherent Zodiac was known to the leaders of ancient cultures, the people in charge of the Mysteries; this is its origin.

* People given admittance to the Mysteries also believed that the Inherent Zodiac is the pathway taken by the soul down into birth, and up into the heavens after death.

* About 500 BC Hellenistic astronomers or astrologers who were associated with the Mysteries, made the fact of the Inherent Zodiac public.

* Ptolemy's writings helped to bring this zodiac into prominence and ensure that it was used for the personal horoscope.

* The Inherent Zodiac was used extensively in the first centuries of Christianity, in Byzantine and European lands, and then later was used by Arabian scholars.

* Each Sign of the Inherent Zodiac is correctly named, because it is linked to the corresponding zodiac constellation. Knowledge of this came from the ancient Mysteries.

* It is misleading to think of the natal chart from Ptolemy as tropical in the sense of seasonal, because it is not. It is an inherent part of the entire Earth's own life-force sphere.

* It was the Inherent Zodiac that was used by the great scientist Johannes Kepler for the approximately 500 charts that he drew up in his work with his clients.[xxv] And it appears that the greatest woman sage of antiquity, Hypatia of Alexandria, used it also.

So, you may have full confidence in the validity and value of the personal horoscope, based on the Inherent Zodiac.

Appendix

The Babylonian text from Prof. Rochberg, complete with technical orthographic markings.

On eclipses of the moon.
Tablet of Anu-bel-sunu, lamentation priest of Anu, son of Nidintu-Anu,
descendant of Sin-leqi-unninni of Uruk. Hand of Anu-[aba-utêr, his son, scri]be of Enuma Anu Enlil of Uruk. Uruk, month I, year 12[1?]
Antiochus III (The Great) [and Antiochus, his son, were kings].
Whoever reveres Anu and Antu [will not remove it (the tablet) in an act of thievery.]
Computational table.
Wisdom of the highest order (lit: of Anu-rank),
exclusive knowledge conc[erning heaven and earth], a secret of the scribal masters.
An expert may show (it) to an[other expert].
A non-expert may not [see it. It is a restriction] of
Anu, Enlil [and Ea, the great gods].

Carl Jung and Origenes
A passage from the Christian scholar Origenes of Alexandria has been used in a book by Carl Jung, to give weight to the validity of the zodiac signs. But in fact this passage is incorrectly presented in Jung's book *Aion*. Origenes says, in a passage directly following on from the words we quoted above,

> Now, the auguries are not discovered by astrologers from the **shape**, but from the mentally-discerned zodiac; though one is not at all able to detect this zodiac (with the senses).[xxvi]
> Yet, let it be that we are even in agreement that the mentally-discerned zodiac signs can be detected. Or, that the truth {about auguries} can be detected from the

sense-perceptible zodiac (the constellations). It is still the case that astrologers admit that they cannot know precisely when a person....(13)

This passage is a rejection of the unwise, fatalistic use of astrology in Christian circles; and this rejection intensified into a general rejection as the centuries went by. It is also clear that Origenes is questioning that since these Inherent Zodiac signs are mentally discerned, whether they can ever be used. He is implying that it is hardly possible to use them. (But today with computers we can identify exactly where their boundaries lie.) So these words show a lack of conviction about either the Inherent Zodiac itself, or the capacity of human being to perceive it. But in Jung's book the initial sentence in this passage from Origenes is greatly distorted and reads like this,

"...yet from that which is conceived only in the mind, and can scarcely, or not even scarcely, be held for certain, the truth of the matter appears." "

This version with its phrase, "the truth of the matter appears" is simply not in the Greek; it is incorrectly translated or just added on.

INDEX

REFERENCES

1 see website: http://www.webexhibits.org/calendars

2 Gavin White, Babylonian Star-lore, Solaria
Publications, London, 2008

3 **Ptolemy** Loeb Classical Library
435, Ptolemy Tetrabiblos

4 See various authorities, e.g., Otto Neugebaur,
The History of Ancient Astronomy;
Problems and Methods, © Astronomical
Society of the Pacific, provided by NASA
Astrophysics Data System /// B. L. Van der
Waerden, Babylonian Astronony III
The earliest astronomical computations,
JSTOR Vol. 10, No. 1 Jan 1951 pp. 20-34

5 Marcus Tullis Cicero, The Dream of Scipio,
trans. P. Bullock, Aquarian Press,
Wellingborough, UK 1983

6, Francesca Rochberg, The Heavenly Writing:
divination, horoscopy and astronomy
in Mesopotamia, Cambridge UP,
UK, 2004

7 Greek text of Valens:
www.hellenisticastrology.com/wiki

8 ΚΛΗΜΕΝΤΟΣ ΤΩΝ ΚΑΤΑ ΑΛΗΘΗ
ΦΙΛΟΖΟΦΙΑΝ ΓΝΩΣΤΙΚΩΝ
ΥΠΟΜΝΗΜΑΤΩΝ ΣΤΟΜΑΤΕΩΝ ΠΡΩΤΟΣ,
Die Griechischen Christlichen
Schriftsteller Leipzig J.C. Hinrichs'che
Buchhandlung, 1906

9 ΠΕΡΙ ΒΙΟΥ ΜΩΥΣΕΩΣ ΛΟΓΟΣ ΤΡΙΥΟΣ
Philonis Judaei Opera Omnis Textus
Editus Lipsiae E. B. Schwickeri 1828
VOL. IV pps. 209-211

10 The Book of Enoch: Pseudepigrapha and Apocrypha of the
Old Testament, in English Vol.2,
edit. R H Charles, OUP 1979

11 Robert Hand On the Invariance of the Zodiac
see http://cura.free.fr/quinq/01hand.html

12 Otto Neugebauer & H.B. van Hoesen, Greek
  Horoscopes, The American Philosophical
  Society, Philadelphia, 1987
13 ΩΡΙΓΕΝΟΥΣ περὶ εἱμαρμένης
  Philocalie 21-27; Sur le Libre arbitre
  p. 191-92, Sources Chretiennes, Paris, 1976

Greek Fonts credit

Picture credits

The Cover,1,2,4,5 : The author's own image-mosaic, but incorporating a photo available freely from the NASA Space agency; namely DE L 252. See,
www.nasa.gov/multimedia/imagegallery
The use of these graphics does not in anyway imply that the owner of these graphics supports or endorses the conclusions of the author expressed in this book.

3 the author

END NOTES

[i] Explained by many authorities, including, van der Waerden, *Babylonian Astronomy, III, the earliest astronomical computations,* in Journal of Near Eastern Studies Jan. 1951
[ii] It is as close to the stars called ξ1, ξ2 and μ Cetus as it is to μ Aries
[iii] Ptolemy' Grk:
 ἄλλων γὰρ ἀρχῶν ὑποτιθεμένων ἢ μηκέτι συγχρῆσθαι ταῖς φυσεσιν αὐτῶν εἰς τὰς προτελέσεις ἀναγκασθνσομεθά ἢ συγχρώμενοι διαπιπτειν παραβάντων καὶ ἀπαλλοτριωθέντων τῶν τὰς δυνάμεις αὐτοῖς ἐμπεριποιησάντων τοῦ ζῳδιακοῦ διαστημάων
[iv] In Greek: dodekataemorios δωδεκατημόριος
[v] Conyers Middleton, The history of the life of Marcus Tullius Cicero p.12
[vi] Cicero, The Dream of Scipio, p. 27, trans. P. Bullock Aquarian Press 1983.
[vii] They called this sign, 'the Hired Man', but they did use a ram as its symbol.
[viii] In Tetrabiblos, Bk.1, Chap. 9, and Bk. 2, Chap. 12

[ix] They had 2 systems, because the Babylonians had 2. That of the astronomer Kidinnu who concluded 8° Aries, and of Naburiannu, who concluded it was 10° Aries.

[x] See his works in the Loeb edition, Book 3.

[xii] Another criticism is whether the qualities attributed to the zodiac signs are a self-supporting illusion right from the start, dreamt up in the Hellenistic age, and have no basis in fact, no support from the qualities associated with the constellations. But the truth is that the ancient star-lore from the Mesopotamian people attributes similar qualities to the 12 constellations, as to the zodiac signs of the same name.

[xiii] This is written in the Preface to Book 7

[xiv] He used the very specific word, mystikos (μυστικός) which means exactly this, not the weaker term *mystic*.

[xv] In Clement's Greek: οἱ δὲ ἐπὶ τῷ στήθει τέτραχα τεταγμένοι δώδεκα τὸν ζῳδιακόν διαγράφουσιν ἡμιν κύκλον κατὰ τὰς τέσσαρας τοῦ ἔτους τροπάς

[xvi] In Clement's Greek: Λέγει τάχα μὲν οὖν τὴν ἀνάστασιν τάχα δὲ ἐκεῖνα αἰνίσσεταί ὡς διὰ τῶν δώδεκα ζῳδίων ἡ ὁδος ταῖς ψυχαῖς γίνεται εἰς τὴν ἀνάληψιν αὐτὸς δὲ καί εἰς τὴν αὐτὴν γίγνεσθαι κάθοδον.

[xvii] The reference to the zodiac signs from the great Origenes of Alexandria (the pupil of Clement) as reported by Carl Jung in his book, Aion, is misleading The text by Origenes does not in fact support the zodiac signs, see Appendix.

[xviii] The Grk of Philo:
ἔπειθ᾽ οἱ κατὰ τὰ στέρνα δώδεκα λίθοι ταῖς χρόαις οὐχ ὅμοιοι διανεμηθέντες εἰς τέσσαρας στοίχους ἐκ τριῶν τίνος ἑτέρου δείγματ᾽ εἰσὶν ἢ τοῦ ζῳδιακοῦ κύκλου; καὶ γὰρ οὗτος τετραχῇ διανεμηθεὶς ἐκ τριῶν ζῳδίων τὰς ἐτησίους ὥρας ἀποτελεῖ ἔαρ θέρος μετόπωρον χειμῶνα τροπὰς τέσσαρας.

[xix] Ptolemy's Greek;
Ὅτι μὲν τοίνυν διαδιδοται καὶ διικνεῖταί τίς δύναμις ὑπὸ τῆς αἰθερώδους καὶ ἀιδίου φύσεως ἐπι πᾶσαν τὴν περιγείαν καὶ δι᾽ ὅλων μεταβλητήν

^{xx} In the Egyptian Mystery text, The Hermetica, there is a passage which reflects this same attitude. It is about the origins of humanity's life-energies, and speaking of the energetic vitality of living beings, it records,"…and from the ether they received their vital spirit." Hermetica edit. Walter Scott, Vol 1, p.122 ....ἐκ δὲ αιθέρος τὸ πνεῦμα ἔλαβον

^{xxi} For example, the influence of the three-sided structure of ice atoms.

^{xxii} Origenes' Grk:
Φέρεται δὴ θεώρημα ἀποδεικνύον τὸν ζωδιακὸν κύκλον ὁμοίως τοῖς πλανωμένοις φέρεσθαι ἀπο᾽ δυσμῶν ἐπὶ ἀνατολὰς δι᾽ ἑκατὸν ἐτῶν μοῖραν
μίαν καὶ τοῦτο τῷ πολλῷ χρόνῳ ἐναλλάτειν τὴν θέσιν τῶν δωδεκατημορίων ἑτέρου μὲν τυγχάνοντος τοῦ νοητοῦ δωδεκατημορίου ἑτέρου τοῦ ὡσανεὶ μορφώματος

^{xxiii} However, Origenes himself did not support astrology for divinatory purposes; so the use of this passage by Jung is incorrect, see Appendix.

^{xxiv} The lunar nodes refer to the points where the pathway of the moon and the sun, around the Earth cross over; they each reveal a zodiac sign of potent importance for the individual.

^{xxv} Kepler never dismissed the Inherent Zodiac, although in his dynamic struggle to understand the cosmos he often threw out various elements of astrology, before taking them back on, perhaps in a new way. He did however write to the English esotericist R. Fludd, about the deep secret of how the soul bears within itself the cosmic elements delineated by the horoscope

^{xxvi} The Grk. here of Origenes:
τὰ δὲ ἀποτελέσματα φασίν εὑρισκεσθαι οὐκ ἐκ τοῦ μορφώματος ἀλλ᾽ ἐκ τοῦ νοητοῦ ζῳδίου· ὅπερ οὐ πάνυ τι δυνατὸν καταλαμβάνεσθαι